RECONSIDERING ARMINIUS

KINGSWOOD BOOKS
Rex D. Matthews, Director
Candler School of Theology, Emory University

EDITORIAL ADVISORY BOARD

Ted Campbell
Perkins School of Theology

Joel B. Green
Fuller Theological Seminary

Richard P. Heitzenrater
Duke Divinity School

Henry Knight III
Saint Paul School of Theology

Mary Elizabeth Mullino Moore
Boston University School of Theology

F. Douglas Powe Jr.
Wesley Theological Seminary

Sam Powell
Point Loma Nazarene University

Karen B. Westerfield Tucker
Boston University School of Theology

Sondra Wheeler
Wesley Theological Seminary

Neil Alexander, ex officio
Abingdon Press

M. Kathryn Armistead, ex officio
Abingdon Press

RECONSIDERING ARMINIUS

BEYOND THE REFORMED AND WESLEYAN DIVIDE

EDITED BY

KEITH D. STANGLIN
MARK G. BILBY
MARK H. MANN

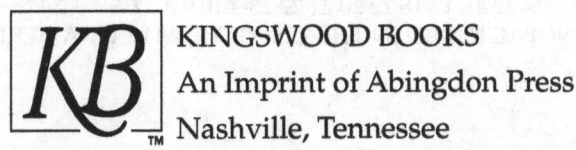

KINGSWOOD BOOKS
An Imprint of Abingdon Press
Nashville, Tennessee

RECONSIDERING ARMINIUS:
BEYOND THE REFORMED AND WESLEYAN DIVIDE
Copyright © 2014 by Abingdon Press

All rights reserved.
No part of this work may be reproduced or transmitted in any form or by any means, electronic or mechanical, including photocopying and recording, or by any information storage or retrieval system, except as may be expressly permitted by the 1976 Copyright Act or in writing from the publisher. Requests for permission should be addressed to Permissions, Abingdon Press, P.O. Box 801, 201 Eighth Avenue South, Nashville, TN 37202-0801 or permissions@abingdonpress.com.

This book is printed on acid-free paper.

Library of Congress Cataloging-in-Publication Data

Reconsidering Arminius : beyond the reformed and Wesleyan divide / edited by Keith D. Stanglin, Mark G. Bilby, and Mark H. Mann.
   pages cm
Includes bibliographical references.
ISBN 978-1-4267-9654-8 (binding: soft back / trade pbk. : alk. paper) 1. Arminianism. 2. Theology, Doctrinal—History—16th century. 3. Theology, Doctrinal—History—17th century. 4. Arminius, Jacobus, 1560-1609. I. Stanglin, Keith D., editor.
BX6195.R425 2014
230'.49—dc23

2014011696

All Scripture quotations unless noted otherwise are taken from the *New Revised Standard Version of the Bible*, copyright 1989, Division of Christian Education of the National Council of the Churches of Christ in the United States of America. Used by permission. All rights reserved.

Scripture quotations marked (AT) are the authors' own translation.

14 15 16 17 18 19 20 21 22 23—10 9 8 7 6 5 4 3 2 1
MANUFACTURED IN THE UNITED STATES OF AMERICA

In memory of Carl Bangs,

who put the historical Harmenszoon back on the scholarly map

CONTENTS

ABBREVIATIONS IX

INTRODUCTION
RECONSIDERING ARMINIUS: RECASTING THE LEGACY XI
    MARK H. MANN AND MARK G. BILBY

CHAPTER 1
CONSECRATED THROUGH SUFFERING: THE OFFICE OF CHRIST IN
THE THEOLOGY OF JACOB ARMINIUS 1
    RICHARD A. MULLER

CHAPTER 2
WAS ARMINIUS AN UNWITTING DETERMINIST? ANOTHER LOOK AT
ARMINIUS'S MODAL LOGIC 23
    THOMAS H. MCCALL

CHAPTER 3
BEYOND LUTHER, BEYOND CALVIN, BEYOND ARMINIUS: THE PILGRIMS
AND THE REMONSTRANTS IN LEIDEN, 1609–1620 39
    JEREMY DUPERTUIS BANGS

CHAPTER 4
THE LOSS OF ARMINIUS IN WESLEYAN-ARMINIAN THEOLOGY 71
    W. STEPHEN GUNTER

CHAPTER 5
JACOB ARMINIUS AND JONATHAN EDWARDS ON THE DOCTRINE
OF CREATION 91
    OLIVER D. CRISP

Chapter 6
Convergence in the "Reformed" Theologies of T. F. Torrance and Jacob Arminius 113
    E. Jerome Van Kuiken

Chapter 7
Was Arminius an Open Theist? Meticulous Providence in the Theology of Jacob Arminius. 137
    John Mark Hicks

Conclusion
Arminius Reconsidered: Thoughts on Arminius and Contemporary Theological Discourse for the Church Today 161
    Keith D. Stanglin

Contributors 169

ABBREVIATIONS

AM	*The Arminian Magazine*, 20 vols. (1778–1797).
C. Bangs	Carl Bangs, *Arminius: A Study in the Dutch Reformation*, rev. ed. (n.p.: F. Asbury Press, 1985).
Dec. sent.	Arminius, *Declaratio sententiae* (1610)
Disp. priv.	Arminius, *Disputationes privatae, de plerisque Christianae religionis capitibus* (1614), in *Opera*, pp. 339–444; *Works*, vol. 2.
Disp. pub.	Arminius, *Disputationes publicae* (1610; Leiden, 2010), in *Opera*, pp. 197–338; *Works*, vol. 2.
Exam. Gom.	Arminius, *Examen thesium D. Francisci Gomari de praedestinatione* ([Amsterdam,] 1645), in *Works*, vol. 3.
Exam. Perk.	Arminius, *Examen modestum libelli, quem D. Gulielmus Perkinsius...edidit* (1612), in *Opera*, pp. 621–777; *Works*, vol. 3.
GCP	Richard A. Muller, *God, Creation, and Providence in the Thought of Jacob Arminius* (Grand Rapids: Baker, 1991).
Gunter	W. Stephen Gunter, *Arminius and His Declaration of Sentiments: An Annotated Translation with Introduction and Theological Commentary* (Waco: Baylor University Press, 2012).
JETS	*Journal of the Evangelical Theological Society* (1969–).
Opera	Arminius, *Opera theologica* (Leiden: Godefridus Basson, 1629).
Stanglin and McCall	Keith D. Stanglin and Thomas H. McCall, *Jacob Arminius: Theologian of Grace* (New York: Oxford University Press, 2012).
Works	Arminius, *The Works of James Arminius: London edition*, trans. James Nichols and William Nichols, 3 vols. (Grand Rapids: Baker, 1986).
YE	Jonathan Edwards, *The Works of Jonathan Edwards*, 26 vols. (Yale University Press, 1957–2008).

IACOBI ARMINII VETERAQVINATIS BATAVI,

SS. Theologiæ Doctoris eximii
OPERA THEOLOGICA.

IN QVIBVS

I. *Orationes: de Sacerdotio Christi: de obiecto, de authore, ac fine, & de certitudine SS. Theologiæ: ac denique de componendo Religionis inter Christianos dissidio.*

II. *Declaratio sententiæ Authoris horum operum de Prædestinatione, prouidentia Dei, libero arbitrio, gratia Dei, Diuinitate Filii Dei, & de Iustificatione hominis coram Deo.*

III. *Apologia aduersus articulos XXXI. in vulgus sparsos.*

IV. *Responsio ad Quæstiones IX. & ad eas Anterotemata.*

V. *Disputationes publicæ & priuatæ.*

VI. *Authoris cum Franc. Iunio de prædestinatione amica collatio: eiusq; ad Theses Iunii de prædestinat. Notæ.*

VII. *Examen modestum prædestinationis Perkinsianæ.*

VIII. *Analysis cap. IX. & Dissertatio in cap. VII. Epistolæ ad Romanos.*

IX. *Epistola ad Hippolytum à Collibus, &c.*

X. *Articuli nonnulli diligenti examine perpendēdi, authoris de præcipuis doctrinæ Christianæ capitibus sententiam plenius declarantes.*

Nunc denuo coniunctim recusa.

PROSTANT
Apud Guilielmum Fitzerum Anglum, Bibliopolam Francofurtanum.

ANNO M.DC.XXXI.

Title page from the second edition of Arminius's collected works. Courtesy of The Leiden American Pilgrim Museum.

Introduction

Reconsidering Arminius: Recasting the Legacy

Mark H. Mann and Mark G. Bilby

Revivalist and theologian Aaron Merritt Hills was one of the most ardent and articulate defenders of Arminianism in late nineteenth- and early twentieth-century America. Hills was raised a Congregationalist and received his theological education first at the feet of revivalist greats such as Charles Finney and Asa Mahan at Oberlin College. He then soaked in the New Light theology while completing his divinity studies at Yale. He would go on to become a successful pastor, evangelist, author, and college president before finally landing among Wesleyan-Holiness folk and becoming one of their chief theological voices of the era.[1] He would conclude his career by serving as a professor of theology at Point Loma Nazarene University (then Pasadena College), where the conference "Rethinking Arminius" was conducted in March of 2012. Several chapters in this volume draw from its presentations. But it is not simply this coincidental institutional connection that makes Hills an interestingly appropriate place to start this book. It is especially what he had to say about Arminius in his magnum opus, the two-volume *Fundamental Christian Theology*, and the way in which his work provides a window into the legacy of Arminianism—a legacy that this collection of essays seeks to recast—that leads us to start with Hills.[2]

At the conclusion to the second volume, Hills includes a brief, two-page outline of the authors of important Christian doctrines for, as he puts it, "the quick use of students."[3] Oddly, of the fourteen persons that he lists, most are heretics, including Sabellius, Arius,

Nestorius, Eutyches, and Socinus. He also mentions Pelagius, and with some sympathy, which makes some sense in light of the little bit he has to say about St. Augustine. He concludes his thoughts about St. Augustine by saying he: "laid the foundation of Calvinism," and thus Hills then has few words to say about Calvin: "developed Calvinism; burned Servetus." In other words, he hardly considers Augustine and Calvin—without question two of the greatest doctors of the Christian church—worth mentioning, still less their ideas.

Hills's sharp condescension toward Calvinism is even more evident elsewhere in his work. In a discussion of the doctrine of unconditional election, he has plenty to say about Calvinism, and not a word of it positive. "Those lovely Calvinists," as he rather sarcastically calls them at times, affirm a doctrine that is "absurd," "insults reason and blasphemes God," "has evil influences," and runs completely "counter to Scripture."[4] In his discussion of the Calvinist penal satisfaction view of the atonement, he has equally dismissive things to say: "the wonder is that any thoughtful, reflective mind can accept it."[5] He is especially aghast that someone as astute as the great Charles Hodge—who serves as Hills's chief Calvinist whipping boy—could affirm that this doctrine is both orthodox and catholic. A bit later, this time in discussing foreordination, Hills provides a rather lengthy quote about what he considers the Calvinist view of God:

> That God unchangeably decreed a universe necessarily so full of wickedness, and involving the unavoidable, eternal, helpless, hopeless doom of so many immortals, that the very thought of it fills any right-thinking soul with horror! The whole idea is a wicked calumny on God.... How that great and good man failed to perceive the *unreasonableness* and *monstrosity* of such theory we cannot understand.[6]

Hills will then go on to conclude,

> Such is Calvinism, the most unreasonable, incongruous, self-contradictory, man-belittling and God-dishonoring scheme of theology that ever appeared in Christian thought. No one can accept its contradictory, mutually exclusive propositions without intellectual self-debasement. For a theologian to flounder about in the morass of its opposing doctrines and assumptions, in a vain attempt to make them harmonize, and then admit that "these are the only

feeble attempts to extricate ourselves from the profundities of theology," is nothing but self-stultification. It holds up a self-centered, selfish, heartless, remorseless tyrant for God, and bids us worship Him.... Thank God [Calvinism] is dying! May its death be hastened. The sooner it breathes its last, the better it will be for the kingdom of God on earth and in heaven.[7]

Hills was clearly not one given to mince words, nor to have any patience with the subtleties in the thought of those at whom he aimed his vitriol.

If the kind of polemic we find in Hills's description of Calvinism seems to us overly harsh, we perhaps might forgive him, for Calvinists were making similar claims about Arminianism. Take, for instance, the great Charles Hodge himself, arguably the most significant Reformed theologian in America since Jonathan Edwards and the primary voice of the so-called "Princeton theology" that would come to define orthodox Calvinism in America. In his most sustained treatment of Arminianism, *Arminianism and Grace*, his core thesis is that Arminianism "in its essential and avowed principles, is subversive of grace."[8] Hodge begins his discussion in a genteel fashion, claiming only to be responding to official and unfair assertions of The Methodist Episcopal Church (which he identifies as the "palladium" of Arminianism in America) that are both unscriptural and immoderate, in hopes of helping them become "more modest in their assaults of Calvinism."[9] While noting certain aspects of Methodist Arminianism that he finds laudable—especially their work among the poor and ability to take the gospel to otherwise unreachable regions through itineracy—Hodge's central focus is demonstrating the extent that Arminians both misunderstand and misrepresent Calvinist theology and themselves profess a theology unworthy of the gospel. Arminianism is couched in "bold" and "dangerous" error, filled with "monstrous absurdities" and "the vilest outrages on truth, decency and honesty."[10] Perhaps even worse, Arminian theology has led Methodism into "practical evils" related to revivalism: sheep stealing and false conversions by which persons are "deluded by mere emotional excitement."[11] Hodge goes on: "It cannot be otherwise. What is false in their system of doctrine and theory of religion, must produce the bitter fruits of evil, just in proportion as it is prominently presented and acted out."[12]

The great irony of the polemical discussions of Arminianism and Calvinism in the work of both Hodge and Hills is the glaring absence of the very figure who stands at the heart of the controversy—Jacob Arminius. Hodge provides extensive treatment of the work of several prominent Arminians—including John Wesley, Wilbur Fisk, and Richard Watson—but not once does he even mention, much less quote or address, the ideas of Arminius himself, despite the fact that the word *Arminianism* shows up multiple times on most pages. As bad as that may be, Hills is not much better. In fact, while mentioning and addressing and citing a number of figures in his several chapters-long defense of Arminianism against Calvinism (most notably Augustine and Calvin) not once is Arminius mentioned or quoted. Of course, he does have something to say about Arminius in his appendix: He was a "martyr to truth" and "founder of Arminianism, the winning theology of the world."[13] Note the depth of the irony here. Hills clearly holds Arminius in high regard, as both the fount of his own dearest theological convictions, and a kind of Christlike martyr-saint. But the actual thought and life of the man are almost completely absent from Hills's work. His words here might be rhetorical, but it is not even apparent that Hills was aware that Arminius was in fact not a martyr, but instead died of tuberculosis a full decade before his condemnation at the Synod of Dort. In fact, in the entirety of the two volumes, Hills only mentions Arminius three times and only quotes him once![14]

We should be careful not to be too critical of either Hills or Hodge in their failure to note Arminius and his theology in their alternative defenses of or attacks upon Arminianism. In truth, Hills and Hodge merely represent the norm when it comes to such polemics, going all the way back to the seventeenth century and continuing well into the twentieth. Arminius the man was either an orthodox saint or a heretical villain, depending on whether one's perspective was that of the Arminian or the Calvinist. Arminius's theology was essentially that rejected at Dort and that affirmed by Arminians ever since.

But contemporary scholarship has begun to paint a very different picture of Arminius's life and thought from that perpetrated in the stereotypes and caricatures that emerged from Dort.

As coeditor Keith Stanglin and contributor Tom McCall have quipped in their 2012 *Jacob Arminius: Theologian of Grace*, we are beginning to gain a much deeper understanding of just how different the "Arminius of faith" is from the "Harmenszoon of history." The decisive shift toward the reconsideration of Arminius began within Arminian circles with Carl Bangs's seminal *Arminius: A Study in the Dutch Reformation* (1971). Bangs's work opened up new horizons for Arminius studies by exploring closely the setting and life of Arminius and detailing the subtleties of Arminius's thought all but ignored in the polemics between Calvinists and Arminians. He thereby demonstrated that much of the so-called Arminian legacy was not as explicitly rooted in the theology of Arminius as previously thought.

Earliest portrait of Arminius, 1609 (reprint, 1625). Courtesy of The Leiden American Pilgrim Museum.

Since the 1990s this refrain has begun to be heard within Reformed circles as well, especially through the work of historical theologian Richard Muller. Muller does not hedge on the fact that certain features of Arminius's theology move away from Calvin and the mainstream Reformed theology of the day. Yet, by comparing their respective treatments of various theological topics, Muller has also shown some deep affinities between Arminius and his Reformed contemporaries.[15] He also warns against the tendency to equate the theology of Arminius with the Arminianism roundly condemned by Reformed theologians since Dort. In the past few years, the reconsideration of Arminius's theology and legacy has continued in the work of a new generation of scholars, including several of the contributors to this book, such as Keith Stanglin, Thomas McCall, and W. Stephen Gunter. Their recent work has given us new insight into Arminius's life and thought. This includes access to previously unpublished works of Arminius and new translations of his writings.

It was to contribute further to such reconsiderations of Arminius's theology and legacy that the editors organized the 2012 conference, "Rethinking Arminius: Wesleyan and Reformed Theology for the Church Today," and assembled this current volume. Indeed, several chapters of this book seek to elucidate further the theology of the historical Harmenszoon and to clarify the ways in which Arminius had essentially been pushed into the background by the time of the Synod of Dort. In chapter one, Richard Muller shows us an Arminius whose theology of the threefold office of Christ was firmly within the mainstream Reformed theology of the day and even anticipated some future developments within Reformed theology on those topics. In a similar vein, in chapter two, Thomas McCall dives into a fairly recent controversy as to whether Arminius might have been an "unwitting determinist." McCall concludes that he was not but reveals to us an Arminius far more the logician and scholastic than many of his theological heirs have realized. In chapter three, Jeremy Bangs shows that the Pilgrim preacher John Robinson, who sojourned in Leiden during the tumultuous decade of the 1610s, in spite of his friendship with leading anti-Arminians, shared Arminian views about the provisionality of human dogmatic statements (such as the Heidelberg Catechism and Belgic Confession. From their defeat, he may have learned the perils of state-controlled religion and of narrowing theology to an alliance with a particular figure (such as Calvin). In chapter four, W. Stephen Gunter traces the disappearance of Arminius's soteriology from among a variety of movements and groups that claimed his mantle: the Remonstrants, the English Arminians, and even the Wesleyan-Arminians.

The second part of the conference title, "Wesleyan and Reformed Theology for the Church Today," sets the stage for the second half of our book. For the past four centuries, Arminius's legacy has been a divisive one. In many respects the name Arminius itself marks a fissure in the Protestant theological tradition that continues to divide the church today. As we planned for the conference, we found ourselves asking, if Arminius has been misunderstood by both Wesleyan-Arminian and Calvinist-Reformed traditions, and his theology might properly be understood as a development *within* rather than *away from* Reformed orthodoxy, might we think of Arminius as a potential bridge, rather than a dividing line, between these two traditions today?

The final three chapters all explore this possibility in different ways. In chapter five, Oliver Crisp compares Arminius to Jonathan Edwards—in many ways the poster boy of resurgent five-point Calvinism—on the doctrine of creation. Crisp surprisingly finds that Arminius's view is far more in line with classical Reformed orthodoxy than Edwards's. In a similar fashion, in chapter six E. Jerome Van Kuiken compares the soteriology of Arminius and that of T. F. Torrance—without question one of the leading Reformed theologians of the twentieth century—and uncovers some striking "convergences" between the two. The analyses of Crisp and Van Kuiken raise the question: If Edwards and Torrance are in some sense the standard bearers for Reformed theology today, is there not also warrant for seeing Arminius as one who has something to offer to contemporary Reformed theology? Finally, in chapter seven, John Mark Hicks explores the question of Arminius's relationship to the contemporary open theism movement. As he notes, this has been a movement especially popular among self-described Arminians who see their work in some sense as a logical outcome of Arminius's. However, Hicks argues, Arminius very clearly was *not* an open theist and embraced a very different understanding of divine providence than do the main proponents of open theism. These forays into historical theology also help show why Classical (Reformed) Arminianism continues to be a live option among those who take Arminius seriously for constructive and confessional theology today.

As that may be, even readers who self-identify with open theism or process theology will find a fascinating precedent in the particular sort of "Arminianism" championed by Conrad Vorstius (as Jeremy Bangs describes in his chapter). On the one hand, this collection represents a dedicated effort to retrieve "the Harmenszoon of history" and discover the contemporary ecumenical potential of rigorous historical theology focused on Arminius. On the other hand, it also helps to trace out the different kinds of Arminianisms that have developed and are still developing, whether Dutch Remonstrant Arminianism or Latitudinarian

Anglican Arminianism, Restorationist Arminianism or Methodist/Wesleyan Arminianism, Classical Arminianism or Open Theist Arminianism. Whether open theism is an authentic expression of Arminianism is debatable, but this volume helps explain *why* it is debatable.

The enigma of multiple Arminianisms can even be seen in the life of Carl Bangs, the father of contemporary Arminius scholarship. As Jeremy Bangs indicated in his conference presentation, his father entered a doctoral program at the University of Chicago with the plan to study process theology. When he got there, his newly arrived advisor, Jaroslav Pelikan, encouraged his (slightly older!) student to continue with the research on Arminius that Bangs had done for his B.D. thesis at Nazarene Theological Seminary. During and after completing his 1958 dissertation ("Arminius and Reformed Theology"), Bangs's affinities for process theology never diminished, although for the rest of his life his scholarly work centered on historical theology and historical biographies.

In many ways, this book is an outgrowth of the life and work of Carl Bangs. Carl inspired his son Jeremy's own affinities for process theology, as well as Jeremy's work on sixteenth- and seventeenth-century Dutch history and thus the history of the American Pilgrims in Leiden. Coeditor Mark Bilby was a teaching assistant for Carl Bangs. Bangs's influence reached many other students and colleagues during his years teaching at Saint Paul School of Theology, Nazarene Theological Seminary, Olivet Nazarene University, and the University of Leiden. Among our editors and contributors, those from the Anglican, Methodist, and Wesleyan-Holiness traditions have certainly felt his influence. Yet, this influence has gone well beyond the denominational settings in which Carl Bangs spent most of his life working. His work has made an impact on persons within the Reformed tradition (including Richard Muller and Oliver Crisp) and Restorationist tradition (including Keith Stanglin and John Mark Hicks), not to mention scholars of sixteenth- and seventeenth-century historical theology more broadly.

This influence does not stem so much from an overt effort on the part of Bangs to do ecumenical theology. Rather, it represents the good fruit of careful historical scholarship. Bangs immersed himself in the study of sixteenth- and seventeenth-century Dutch language, culture, and history. He sought out unused and previously unknown primary source texts, crawling under houses (!)

and pillaging bookstores across Europe for academic treasures related to Arminius. Out of respect for his subject matter, he weighed the evidence carefully and refused to be swayed by the sorts of caricatures of Arminius—whether positive or negative—that burdened later polemics. He was rightly annoyed by the casual use of the name of Arminius—whether to lionize or to vilify him—by persons who had never bothered to read him. On the one hand, he practiced scholarship in the service of the church. On the other hand, he did not allow his scholarly conclusions to be predetermined by any particular church or fixed statement of beliefs.

Simply put, Carl Bangs was a gifted church historian. The "Rethinking Arminius" conference, which took place nearly ten years after Carl's death (July 7, 2002), was dedicated to his memory, as is this volume. The editors hope that it honors him well.

NOTES

1. For a recent exploration of Hills's life and thought, see C. J. Branstetter, *Purity, Power, and Pentecostal Light: The Revivalist Doctrine and Means of Aaron Merritt Hills* (Eugene, Oreg.: Pickwick, 2012).

2. A. M. Hills, *Fundamental Christian Theology: A Systematic Theology*, 2 vols. (Pasadena, Calif.: C. J. Kinne, 1931).

3. Ibid., 2:433–34.

4. Ibid., 2:152–64.

5. Ibid., 2:76.

6. Ibid., 2:139, italics original.

7. Ibid., 2:148, 151.

8. Charles Hodge, *Arminianism and Grace* (Toronto: James Bain, 1861), 6. This pamphlet originally appeared as an article, "Arminianism and Grace," *Princeton Review* 28, no. 1 (1856): 38–59.

9. Hodge, *Arminianism and Grace*, 5–6.

10. Ibid., 8–10.

11. Ibid., 31.

12. Ibid.

13. Hills, *Fundamental Christian Theology*, 1:310.

14. Ibid., 1:298.

15. See, for instance, *GCP*.

CHAPTER 1

CONSECRATED THROUGH SUFFERING: THE OFFICE OF CHRIST IN THE THEOLOGY OF JACOB ARMINIUS

Richard A. Muller

ARMINIUS'S APPROACH TO THE OFFICE OF CHRIST: ISSUES AND CONTEXTS

The doctrine of Christ's threefold office was not a matter of major debate among Protestant theologians of the early modern era, even though various more or less subordinate topics such as the extent of Christ's satisfaction received intense scrutiny. Although its basic formulation and subsequent prominence as a doctrinal topic in the *Loci communes*, gathered *Disputationes*, and theological *Institutiones* of the era can probably be traced to the final edition of Calvin's *Institutes*, the concept of Christ's office and even the distribution of the office under the titles of prophet, priest, and king was not original to Calvin and, indeed, had a long history in the thought of the church, extending back as far as Eusebius of Caesarea in the early fourth century.[1] Arminius's doctrine of the threefold office fits well into this post-Reformation development, and it also provides a basis for shedding some light on the perennial question of Arminius's relationship to the Reformed tradition.

THE OFFICE OF CHRIST: ARMINIUS'S BASIC ASSUMPTIONS

The Nature of Religion, Covenant, and the Office of Christ

Arminius's understanding of the doctrine of Christ's threefold office was largely uncontroversial. The sole exception is the hint of subordination of the Son to the Father in Arminius's statements concerning the imposition of Christ's office and his consecration to the office, although neither Arminius's oration on Christ's priestly office nor his disputations on the office of Christ caused the debate—nor were they referenced in it.[2] More significant than the potentially controversial element, however, are the connections drawn by Arminius among the fundamental relationship between God and human beings that is constitutive of religion, the foundational identification of true religion as covenantal,[3] and the basic functions of covenantal religion—the kingly, prophetic, and priestly—as adumbrating both the necessity of Christ's mediation and the threefold form of Christ's office as prophet, priest, and king. This rather prominent covenantal aspect of Arminius's Christology is evident both in his *Oration on the Priesthood of Christ* and in his *Public Disputation* on Christ's offices. It places him in a significant relation to developments in the Reformed theology of his time, specifically to the development of the doctrine of the *pactum salutis* or eternal covenant of redemption between the Father and the Son, a relationship noted by William Ames and Herman Witsius, among others.[4]

The oration on Christ's priestly office begins with a set of general observations that Arminius identifies as necessary to the understanding of Christ's office as such and that provide the basis for understanding aspects of the office—notably the kingship and priesthood of Christ. The relationships that subsist between God and human beings all begin with a divine act that involves something bestowed by God and received by human beings. What is also required, however, for there to be a full relationship between God and human beings is human response—specifically an act that has its "beginning" (*initium*) in human beings and its end in God. The language here reflects the standard definition of religion found in the Protestant theology of Arminius's day, namely, the bond between God and human beings consisting in true knowledge and worship, and Arminius's own summary statement that "religion is the duty of a human being toward God" as defined by God's word and as exercised in worship.[5]

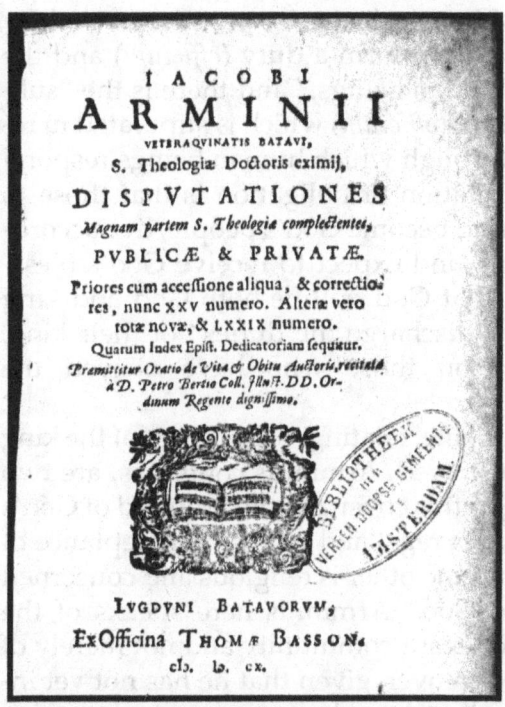

The title page from the 1610 edition of Arminius's *Disputations*. Courtesy of The Leiden American Pilgrim Museum.

Human beings ought, in other words, to acknowledge the divine act and respond with gratitude. Such gratitude is a debt owed to God, to be paid as demanded and determined by God as the giver of the gift. Yet God has also, in kindness and generosity (*benignitas*) established this relationship of act and response as a "mutual covenant."[6] The covenant is such that God first manifests God's obligation to humanity before human beings begin to consider themselves as obligated to God.

Here again, in addition to the significant parallels and commonalities between Arminius's thought on covenant and the developing Reformed theologies of his time, we may have a hint of arguments that would later separate Arminius's theology from that of his Reformed colleagues. Where the larger number of Reformed writers would declare that, given both the divine omnipotence and the utter freedom of God in conferring the good being on his creatures, God is under no obligation to creation and certainly does not find God's power limited by the existence of the created order, Arminius disagreed, perhaps reflecting an understanding of the traditional language of "ordained power" (*potentia ordinata*) and arguing that the act of creating was a self-limiting act and that the divine right over creatures was defined and delimited by the act of creation. The act of creation, in turn, is the basis of God's right to require religion of human beings,[7] and this religion, rightly understood, takes the form of covenant.

Still, Arminius's basic definition of covenant is quite conformable to the Reformed approaches of the era. Arminius argues that all covenants made between God and human beings have two fundamental parts or elements. There is the "prior promise of God, by which [God] obliges himself to perform a duty (*officium*) and the acts corresponding to it for human beings," and there is the "subsequent prescription of the duty (*officium*) which is stipulated in return for human beings and through which human beings respond mutually to God."[8] The stipulation or obligation is that those to whom the covenant is proposed become God's people, live according to God's commandments, and expect to receive God's blessings. The divine promise is that God will be both God and king to the people, will properly "discharge the duties" of their king, and will bestow blessings on those who have obeyed the commandments.

Associated with the divine rule, relating to the duties of the king and to the blessings to be bestowed, Arminius continues, are two primary functions belonging to this covenant and required of God's people. One primary function is regal and related to acceptance of supreme authority of God, and the other is religious and concerned with devoted submission to God.[9] Arminius here speaks of the functions belonging to the covenant community and not merely of the divine office or offices. Moreover, given that he has not yet introduced the problem of the fall and that he assumes a prelapsarian as well as a postlapsarian covenant, these religious functions or duties are embedded in the fabric of creation itself. Regal and religious (or priestly) duties arise directly from the covenantal relationship (*ex foederatione*): Under the regal function, God's people engage in giving thanks and in making requests of the authority; under the religious function, they follow their calling for the sake of sanctification and, constituted as priests of God, perform the services of offering gifts and prayers. Arminius also includes the prophetic function, albeit as a subset of the kingly, given that prophecy is "nothing other than an announcement of the royal will."[10] All three of these functions arise directly out of the covenant. There is also precedent in the religious activities of the ancient patriarchs for the union of the priestly and kingly offices—a union made most clear in the person of Melchizedek.[11]

Arminius is also quite clear in noting the incompleteness and utter insufficiency of the historical enactments of these offices, given the failure of the entire human race in Adam. There was a "constant and perpetual" will of God that religious observance and covenant be maintained. He identifies Adam as "first human being and [first] priest"—and in both capacities the federal representative of the human race.[12] The fall of Adam not only broke covenant with God and left both Adam and his entire progeny locked in sin, but it also defiled religious observance and deprived humanity of the right to proper priestly office.[13] The argument here assumes a significant background in the reading of the Genesis narrative: that Adam was not only the first human being but also the first priest. This relates to the ancient understanding of the trees in the garden as sacramental and as the focal points of religious observance in the original, unfallen economy. Given, moreover, the Pauline Adam-Christ parallel, it was not at all curious for Arminius to develop this point and incorporate it into an argument leading toward the identification of Christ's office, particularly in its priestly aspect, as the necessary fulfillment of God's plan for human religion.

The Imposition of Office

Several issues can be noted here, particularly with reference to the language of "calling" and "imposition." First, when Arminius references Christ's calling to and imposition of the office, he is not making a further Ramistic division of the topic into two distinct acts, calling and imposition. Rather, he is using the two terms as identifications of the same act. Further, Arminius's language has reference to Christ's divine as well as his human nature. In this vein, calling may more clearly reference Christ's humanity. In any case, Arminius consistently references the entire person of Christ, constituted as Mediator, and therefore as both divine and human, considered in the economy of salvation. Even when referring to the roles of the Father and the Son in the constitution of the priestly office, Arminius makes consistent reference to the Son as Christ and Mediator rather than to the Son as second person of the Trinity in eternity.[14]

This language of imposition, moreover, points in two directions. On the one hand, specifically with reference to the imposition of office, Arminius offers a distinctly covenantal reflection in his *Oration on the Priesthood of Christ*, a reflection that was noted among the Reformed writers of the seventeenth century, notably William Ames, as a significant anticipation of the doctrine of the *pactum salutis*, or covenant of redemption, that attained prominence among the Reformed beginning in the fourth decade of the seventeenth century.[15] On the other hand, there is a somewhat subordinationist accent in this language of imposition that carried over quite clearly into later Remonstrant theology, notably the theology of Philip van Limborch.[16] Arminius elaborates on these issues in a series of comments on the imposition of Christ's office.

There are three parts to the discussion of the imposition of office, the third of which concerns us here. This third point, the mode of imposition (*impositio*), enjoining (*iniunctio*), or undertaking (*susceptio*), returns Arminius to the issue of covenant, inasmuch as the Levitical priesthood of the Old Testament was imposed by God in the form of a covenant, as described in Malachi 2:5, "My covenant of life and peace is with him" (AT) (*Pactum meum est cum illo vitae & pacis*). We may hypothesize that Arminius's choice of *pactum* is explained by the following statement, that the covenant inaugurating the priesthood of Christ was a particular kind of covenant, namely one confirmed by "the taking of an oath" (*juramentum*).[17]

In any case, Arminius, like a large number of the early modern Reformed writers, argued a special, indeed, a foundational covenant relationship between God, specifically God the Father, and Christ as mediator. Also in accord with the general tendency of Reformed thought in his time he identified it as a *pactum*, not as a *foedus*. Ames similarly defined Christ's calling (*vocatio*) to his office as "the action (*actio*) of God, preeminently of the Father, by which a special covenant (*singulari quodam pacto*) being inaugurated, the Son was destined to his office."[18]

This covenantal relationship between God the Father and Christ as mediator was clearly of considerable importance to Arminius, inasmuch as he also referenced it in one of his other inaugural orations at Leiden, the *Oration on the Object of Theology*, and again in one of his *Private Disputations*. In the *Oration on the Object of Theology* he argued the necessity of a new and gracious covenant, enabled by the "intervention of a mediator," and he identified Christ as the "appointed" mediator who "obediently undertook the office imposed on him by the Father."[19] A few pages later in the same oration

Arminius comments that faith in Christ is necessary not only on the basis of God's decree (*ex decreto Dei*) but also on the basis of the promise (*ex promissione*) made by Christ to the Father, specifically on the basis of the covenant (*ex pacto*) enacted between them.[20] On the part of God the Father, the covenant consisted in the requirement of an act and a promise of reward. On the part of Christ as priest, it consisted in an acceptance of the promise and a further offer or promise to perform the act. As Arminius later indicates, this act would necessarily be "voluntary and pure."[21]

In the *Private Disputation*, Christ's redemptive work as priest and king is defined as being "constituted" by God and as made effective among human beings through the right performance of religion. As in his *Oration on the Priesthood of Christ*, Arminius understands religion as covenantal and in the *Private Disputations* specifically argues that the divine command to worship rightly, as made possible through the work of Christ, is presented as a covenant containing stipulations and promises.[22] These stipulations and promises made between God and believers in their covenant of grace, or "new covenant," reflect what Arminius had also indicated of the covenant or pact between the Father and Christ. In other words, Arminius's understanding of the new covenant rests on his framing of the covenant between the Father and Christ as mediator. Thus, "the stipulation on the part of God and Christ is, that God shall be God and Father in Christ, if in the name, and by the command of God, [a person] acknowledges Christ as his Lord and Savior, that is, if he believes in God through Christ and in Christ, and if he offers love, worship, honor, fear, and complete obedience as prescribed."[23] And,

> the promise on the part of God the Father and of Christ, is, that God will be the God and Father, and that Christ, through the administration of his sacerdotal and regal offices, will be the Savior of those who have faith in God the Father and in Christ, and who offer faith and the obedience to God the Father and Christ, that is, he will accept the performance of religious duty, and will reward it.[24]

He approaches the issue from the rather traditional perspective often followed in Reformed circles of reproducing the basic Anselmic argument for the necessity of a divine-human mediator with minor variation. In short, the high priestly sacrifice required for salvation would necessarily be performed by a single person and, in the form taken by Arminius's argument, the movement from figure or type to full reality required that the same one be "both priest and sacrifice."[25] The priest and the sacrifice would need to be human in order rightly to expiate the sins of human beings, but no human being could possibly perform such an act given the sinfulness of the human race and the inability of sinners to stand before God in any capacity. In the divine wisdom, therefore, the mediator was decreed to be one who would be "born in the likeness of sinful flesh, and yet without sin." The "dignity," however, of such an office was so great that "even man in his pure state" would be incapable of fulfilling the task. "Therefore the Word of God, who from the beginning was with God, and by whom the worlds, and all things visible and invisible, were created, ought himself to be made flesh, to undertake the office of the priesthood, and to offer his own flesh to God as a sacrifice for the life of the world."[26] The person capable of the task, therefore, is "Jesus Christ, Son of God and [son] of man," and it is with Christ that God the Father makes his special covenant of redemption.[27]

These formulations, taken together, offer some indication of the relatively unusual way in which Arminius construed the problem of the relationship of Christ to both covenant and divine decree—which brings us to the second issue, namely, the implications of Arminius's language of imposition of office as distinct from "designation" or "ordination." This terminology also marks a significant point of consistency in Arminius's formulations. From his earliest comments on the issue in his oration to his later disputations on the subject, Arminius maintained the language of the "imposition" of office. By contrast, in his earlier disputation on the subject, Gomarus, echoing Ursinus, had specifically used the term *ordination*, identifying Christ's "anointing" (with reference to Matt 17:5) as the "ordination of the Son of God to the office of highest Prophet, Priest, and King."[28]

The implication of this difference in terminology is clarified by its parallel in Arminius's doctrine of predestination, specifically in his definition of the first absolute decree of God as "that by which he decreed to appoint his Son, Jesus Christ, for a Mediator, Redeemer, Saviour, Priest, and King, who might destroy sin by his own death, might by his obedience obtain the salvation which had been lost, and might communicate it by his own virtue."[29] Here also, focus is on Christ the Mediator and not on either the Son as second person of the Trinity or on a distinction of the two natures in Christ. In both places, Arminius consistently addresses the issue of mediation. In the discussion of the imposition of office, the person referenced is the divine-human person of the mediator. In the similar definition of the decree, the divine person of the Son is referenced only in relation to his incarnate work as mediator. From the contemporary Reformed perspective, the problem with this language was not so much with what was present in the definition but with what was absent, namely, an insistence on the coequality of Father and Son as God in the foundation or act of decreeing the salvation of humanity.

THE PROPHETIC OFFICE

In his *Public Disputation* on the subject, Arminius discusses each of the offices according to the same fourfold pattern of exposition. First, he argues that the office, as imposed, belongs to Christ; second, he explains the nature (*qualitas*) of the office; third, he outlines its functions or performance (*functiones*) and confirmation (*confirmatio*); and fourth, he discusses the result (*eventus*) of the office.[30] From a formal or methodological perspective, this careful parsing and division of the subject belongs to the scholastic character of the disputation. In other words, he grounds the functions or acts in the prior identification of the thing and its nature and the effects or results in the functions or acts arising from the nature. It should also be noted that this model of imposition, nature, function and confirmation, and result or consequence carried over into the theology of Limborch.[31]

The Messiah, Christ, was the "future Prophet promised to the fathers in the Old Testament."[32] Arminius lines out various prophecies from Moses's words in Deuteronomy ("The LORD your God will raise up for you a prophet," Deut 18:15), to the prophecies of Isaiah (among them, "I have given you as a covenant to the people, a light to the nations," Isa 42:6). Such texts were fulfilled in Christ, who could cite Isaiah and then say, "Today this scripture has been fulfilled" (Luke 4:21). What is more, Christ was clearly called by God to the prophetic office, as also predicted by Isaiah, "The Spirit of the Lord GOD is upon me, because the LORD has anointed me" (Isa 61:1).[33]

The nature of the office is to be understood from Christ's calling and the divine "imposition" of office, the preparation (*instruc-*

tio) for the office, and the divine assistance provided him, but also from the teaching (*doctrina*) presented by Christ.[34] Christ's calling or his being sent (*missio*) was approved by God with the signs of the heavens opening, the Spirit descending in the form of a dove, and the voice of God the Father. Christ's preparation for the office was, moreover, higher than that of the prophets of the Old Testament, given that it was not accomplished by means of dreams or visions, angelic visitation, or even verbal communication, but by the "clear vision of God" and an "intimate knowledge [*intimum intuitum*] of the secrets of the Father," supported by the continuous presence of the Holy Spirit, as testified by the Gospel according to John.[35]

Beside these indicators of the nature and character of Christ's prophetic office stands the "object" of Christ's office, known through the "excellence of the teaching" (*Doctrinae excellentia*). For in his prophetic office Christ did not proclaim the law either as a promise of salvation to those who would be capable of paying their debt to God or as the confirmation of sin and condemnation. Nor was Christ's office merely the announcement of a gracious promise of righteousness and salvation to those who believe, as given to Abraham. Rather Christ's office announced the gospel itself, indeed presented (*exhibuit*) the grace and truth of the gospel as the end of the law and the accomplishment of the promise.[36]

There is both a common ground and a difference here between Arminius's definition and the approach of his Reformed contemporaries. Ursinus's and Gomarus's definitions of the prophetic office similarly indicate that it is the revelation of the redemptive will of God toward humanity through the external preaching of the gospel, accompanied by inward illumination and an efficacy of teaching,[37] but—where Arminius's definition of the office pointed solely toward the soteriological ends or goals of the office—Gomarus's definition (perhaps expectedly, given the supralapsarian direction of his thought) noted these ends as penultimate or subordinate to the highest end, namely, the glory of God.[38] Bucanus, similar to Arminius, argued that the object of Christ's prophetic office was not law, but gospel, but he went on to define the gospel as the revelation of "the secret counsel of the Father concerning the redemption of humanity, by the Word, the Holy Spirit, and the sacraments, both by himself and also by ministers of the Word."[39] In both cases, whether the larger causal framework of Gomarus's definition or the Trinitarian approach to the decree found in Bucanus's definition of the office, there is a correlation with the Reformed tendency to reference the role of the second person of the Trinity in ultimate terms, as compared with the more subordinationistic tendency of Arminius's language.

There is also a significant connection noted by Arminius between the prophetic and the priestly office. The effect or result of Christ's prophetic office was the conversion of a few and the rejection of his teaching by the greater number of his hearers, leading to his condemnation, crucifixion, and death. In as much as God foreknew this result, Arminius concludes that the prophetic office itself was ordained by God to lead toward "the consecration of Christ through sufferings" and thereby serve as a prologue to the priestly office. This argument certainly marks a different approach than that of Ursinus, who identified the connection among the offices as a prophetic or teaching function that belonged to the priests of the Old Testament.[40]

THE PRIESTLY OFFICE OF CHRIST

Christ's Preparation for Office

The preparation for office, as argued by Arminius in his *Private Disputations*, is a series of four acts, each with a twofold purpose: Christ was prepared as both Priest and sacrifice. His preparation for the priesthood itself consisted in four distinct acts: first, the calling (*vocatio*) to or imposition (*impositio*) of the office; second, the sanctification and consecration of his person by the Holy Spirit; third, his obedience (*obedientia*) and sufferings (*passiones*); and fourth, "in a certain respect" his being revived from the dead.[41]

The bestowal of office, considered both as calling and (most characteristically) as imposition, was crucial to Arminius's understanding of Christ's priestly work. It reflects some of the concerns he expressed against the similar exposition of the ordination of the Mediator in William Perkins's treatise on predestination. Arminius could argue that, simply given the "excellence" or eminence of Christ's person, Christ would have been worthy of worship, but beyond this excellence two further things were necessary for Christ to be the proper "object of Religion (*Religionis objectum*)."[42] Arminius had raised this issue in previous disputations.

The object of Christian religion is that toward which the faith and worship of a religious person ought to tend. This object is God and God's Christ. God principally, Christ subordinately under God; God *per se*, Christ as God had constituted him the object of this religion.[43] "We have treated of God, who is the first object of the Christian religion: and now we treat of Christ, who, next to God, is another object of the same religion.... God is the object of the Christian religion, not only as Creator, but also as Re-creator; in which latter respect Christ also, as constituted by God to be the savior, is the object of the Christian religion."[44] It is worth noting that this understanding of the object of Christian religion and, therefore, of theology as well, does not fit easily into the rather glib twentieth-century characterizations of theologies as "theocentric" or "christocentric."

Arminius develops his point by identifying the two things necessary for Christ to be a proper object of worship: first that Christ undertake various offices for the sake of the salvation of humanity and second that Christ should have dominion over all things bestowed on him by the Father.[45] Taken together these two things identify Christ as Savior and Mediator. As Savior he embodies the goal or end both of the offices and of the dominion given to him; as Mediator he is the one who undertakes the work that brings about that end. It is his specific mediatorial work of acquiring salvation that is the object of his priestly office.[46] This priesthood, moreover, is not "according to the order of Levi" but according to that of Melchizedek, who was both "priest of the Most High God" and "King of Salem."[47]

The second issue raised by Arminius in consideration of Christ's preparation for the priestly office is the sanctification and consecration of Christ's person. After being called and having the office conferred or imposed, the person must be rendered suitable for the office. In all of his discussions of the topic, Arminius is clear that it was not sufficient that Christ, as Mediator, be a divine-human person and that his humanity be conceived like all human beings except for sin. This is certainly the necessary foundation, but there also must be a further sanctification and consecration of the person as a requisite to the fulfillment of the office, resting on the work of the Holy Spirit and arising from the obedience and suffering of Christ. This consecration to the priestly office, moreover, would necessarily be paralleled by a preparation of Christ as sacrifice—by obedience and by "separation," given that the sacrifice must be holy.[48]

The Nature and Quality of Christ's Priesthood: The Type and the Antitype

As the true priest and not merely a type of the priesthood, Christ was "at once both priest (*sacerdos*) and sacrifice (*victima*) in one person." The language, here, probably demands some explanation: Arminius contrasts the *sacerdos verus* with a *sacerdos typicus*. As he argues in all of his discussions of the priestly office, the Old Testament priesthood was the "type," namely, the figure or sign of the true priesthood that was to come. Many of Arminius's hearers and readers would have recognized this argument as dependent on Ursinus's exposition of the Heidelberg Catechism where the anointing of Christ to his office is distinguished from a typical, ceremonial, or sacramental anointing as one that is both "real" and "spiritual."[49]

Arminius goes on to identify a series of differences between the Levitical and the messianic priesthood that illustrates the superiority and preeminence of the latter. Here, too, there are resemblances to Ursinus's exposition.[50] Thus, as is often indicated concerning the distinction between the old covenant or testament and the new, the Levitical priesthood was typical and shadowy (*typicum* and *umbratile*), the messianic priesthood a full reality truly presented (*reale* and *verum*) as an "express image."[51] In the Levitical priesthood, moreover, priest and sacrifice "differed in subject," inasmuch as the priest offered sacrifices presented by others. But in the messianic priesthood, the priest offers himself in the true expiatory priestly act. The Old Testament priesthood, then, is a type or figure that only partially fulfilled the requirement of redemption—by implication, because the priest was only the officiant and not also sacrificial victim. The true priesthood of the New Testament, promised or foreshadowed in the type, does fulfill the requirement of redemption by combining officiant and sacrifice into a single office—thereby fulfilling and completing once for all the work of the priesthood. The sacrificial death of the true priest, moreover, fulfills the requirement of the satisfaction theory of atonement to which Arminius, like virtually all of his Protestant contemporaries, subscribed. The sin of the first human being and head of the human race had to be expiated by the payment of its penalty, death, by the only kind of being capable of making the human payment.

Christ's Performance of His Office

As typically argued in his time, Arminius understood the performance or discharge of Christ's priestly office as consisting of two parts: Christ's sacrifice and his intercession. This was clearly the view of Calvin, and it had remained standard fare among the Reformed writers of Arminius's time and afterward.[52] Arminius adds that the blessing, performed by both priests and kings of the Old Testament, belongs more properly to the communication of salvation and, therefore, to the effects or gifts that follow the fulfillment of Christ's office rather than to its performance.[53] Again there is a clear reflection of Ursinus's discussion, with the primary difference being the exclusion, from Arminius's discussion, of the work of teaching.

The sacrifice or, to use Arminius's phrase, the "offering of an expiatory sacrifice," was necessarily preceded by a preparation consisting in privation and suffering, identified elsewhere by Arminius as taking place during Christ's initial exercise of his prophetic office and as serving as a consecration to his priesthood. This preparation being accomplished, the offering of his self-sacrifice was in two parts, confirming the reality, finality, and utter sufficiency of Christ's work: namely, both an earthly and a heavenly part. In the earthly part of his offering, namely the sacrifice itself, Christ shed his blood "on the altar of the cross" and in his death suffered the punishment for sin, thereby paying the price of redemption. This part of his offering was necessarily earthly and outside of the heavenly "holy of holies" inasmuch as there is no shedding of blood and no presence of death and its power in heaven. As a second part of the offering, Christ presented his resurrected body in heaven, "sprinkled with the blood he shed," as a sign or symbol set before the divine majesty of the price paid for the redemption of humanity. These two acts of offering, therefore, correspond with the two states of Christ's person, the first belonging to his state of humiliation, the second to his state of exaltation—the first completed by the sanctifying work of the Holy Spirit in his obedience, the second further consecrating his person in the sprinkling of his blood.[54]

It is perhaps useful to note here that Arminius's sense of two functions, one sacrificial, the other intercessory, belonging to Christ's office is also a standard feature of the early modern Reformed doctrine of Christ's work. The significant difference was that Christ's intercessory prayer was generally interpreted by the Reformed as confirming the limitation of the efficacy of Christ's sacrifice or satisfaction to the elect, whereas Arminius states that Christ's intercession is for "believers." Nonetheless, Arminius's formulation, if considered apart from his doctrine of predestination, makes virtually the same point as the Reformed. "Christ," he writes, "is said to intercede for believers, to the exclusion of the world," even though he had "offered a sacrifice sufficient to take away the sins of all humanity," not all of whom have confidence in God or remain steadfast to the end.[55] Arminius was, after all, not a universalist.

Arminius concludes this section of his *Oration* by returning to the covenantal theme, specifically the theme of the *pactum* between the Father and the Son: Christ, who had in effect taken a covenantal oath to fulfill his office and fulfilled it completely, receives the Father's response. The priesthood of Christ will continue forever and Christ himself will be "elevated to regal dignity." All power in heaven and on earth is given to him, and he is fully revealed as the "priest forever after the order of Melchizedek," given that Melchizedek was both priest and king.[56]

THE KINGLY OFFICE

The theme of Christ's consecration through suffering marks the beginning of Arminius's treatment of the kingly office and indicates—as confirmed by his subsequent disputation on the two estates of Christ—his close association of Christ's kingship with his exaltation to the right hand of the Father.[57] Because of his full performance of the duties of the priestly office, Christ was given "regal dignity" by the Father and all of the other gifts requisite to the bestowal of salvation on believers. Arminius defined the kingly office as "a mediatorial function, by which, the Father having constituted him Lord over all things which are in heaven and in earth, and peculiarly the King and the head of his church, he governs all things and the church, to her salvation and the glory of God."[58] At the end of the definition, he adds, "We will view this office in accommodation to the church, because we are principally concerned in this consideration," thereby removing what he called the "cosmic" or universal aspects of Christ's kingly rule from consideration.[59]

In the *Private Disputations*, once his definition is in place, Arminius proceeds, as before, to his discussion first of the "functions" or "acts" of the office and then of its result or consequences. The functions of Christ's kingly office are four: vocation or calling, lawgiving, the communication of blessings, and judgment.[60] Paralleling the prophetic office, there is the function or work of calling, here more specifically defined not so much as the teaching of the gospel but as calling to "participation" in Christ's kingdom, consisting in the call to repent and believe the gospel. To this, Arminius adds what could be understood as a covenantal element given that he describes the call in terms not simply of promise but of both reward and threat—namely, the reward of participation in the kingdom and the threat of eternal separation from the presence of the Lord.[61] The king—his second function—is also a proposer and maker of law (*legislator*), who prescribes duties and conjoins sanctions of reward and punishment for performance and nonperformance, for the sake of the conduct of his kingdom.

As a third function of his kingly office, Christ bestows blessings on his people. These include not only the primary benefits of the remission of sins and the inward gracious witness of the Spirit to believers' adoption but also illumination of the mind, strength against temptation, and a new or renewed inscription of the law of God in the heart. Christ's fourth and final kingly function or act is his passing of judgment "justly without respect of persons" on all the thoughts and acts of human beings to the end of final reward and final punishment.[62] This legal emphasis, which runs through Arminius's understanding of the kingly office, most probably connects with his strongly covenantal approach to religion and its required offices, given that covenants have stipulations and duties, rewards and punishments. This understanding of kingly rule and its laws is quite similar to that found among his Reformed contemporaries, notably, Trelcatius and Gomarus.[63]

SOME CONCLUSIONS

Armimius's doctrine of the office of Christ belongs, as do most of the doctrinal topics on which he elaborated, to the early orthodox phase of Reformed theology and remains best understood in the context of the theological developments of the era. His thought has clear antecedents in and affinities with the theology of such varied

Reformed thinkers of the era as Calvin, Vermigli, Ursinus, Bucanus, Junius, Gomarus, and Trelcatius—affinities that remain even when Gomarus and Trelcatius are numbered among the opponents of his theology in the debates that ultimately led to the Synod of Dort. Arminius studied in Leiden and Geneva, preached in Amsterdam, and had returned to Leiden as a full professor; both his training and the locations of his ministerial and professorial service were Reformed. The pronounced covenantal background of his thought on Christ's office, whether in its assumption of a prelapsarian covenant with Adam, of a postlapsarian covenant reestablishing the relationship between God and the human race after the fall, or of a further, special covenant between God the Father and Christ the Mediator, reflects the nonpolemical, ecclesially or confessionally internal developments of Reformed theology in Arminius's time.

Apart from the consistent reflection of his Reformed roots and context, most significant about Arminius's teaching on the office of Christ are the points on which his elaborations of the doctrine yielded distinctive characteristics. Here we can count Arminius's emphasis on the foundation of the offices in covenant, covenant in the nature of religion itself, and religion in the order of creation. Beyond this, certainly his emphasis on Christ's consecration to his office in and through his work, notably in his suffering, adds a significant dimension to the doctrine—indeed it provides the linkage in the work of Christ itself between his prophetic and his priestly office as well as between the priestly and the kingly office. The union of divinity and humanity was, of course, complete in incarnation, but entrance into the fullness of the office depended, in Arminius's view, in large part on the obedience, patience, and endurance of Christ according to his humanity. Subordination to the task, perhaps also given emphasis by Arminius's insistence on the covenantal subordination of the Son to the Father, underlined in Arminius's thought the proximity of Christ to the human race as a ground of faith and hope.

Most of Arminius's definitions and formulations have identifiable roots in the Reformed tradition, some in Calvin's formulation of the threefold office, and a greater number in Ursinus's exposition of the Heidelberg Catechism. A large part of these definitions and formulations, moreover, find distinct parallels in the thought of Arminius's immediate colleagues at Leiden, Trelcatius and Gomarus, as well as in the thought of other Reformed contemporaries such as Bucanus and Scharpius. On the basis of these roots and parallels, it is safe to conclude that Arminius's understanding of Christ's office parallels and generally reflects the fairly standard Reformed paradigms of the era. The absence of complaint in his own time concerning this aspect of his doctrine, even from his angriest opponents, confirms the conclusion. We can note his distinction between Christ's sacrifice and intercession was typical of the Reformed, as was his basic satisfaction theory of atonement. So also his adumbration of the *pactum salutis* places him in the line of early Reformed development—although the subordinationist tendencies noted particularly in Arminius's language of the "imposition" of Christ's office look more toward Episcopius and later Remonstrant theology. The conclusion, then, on the issue of Arminius's relation to the Reformed tradition, when argued in terms of his approach to the office of Christ, is that he stood in large part within the tradition, contributing to the lines of development of the tradition evident in the early seventeenth century. Yet there were also a few divergences in his thought that pointed more toward later Remonstrant theology.

NOTES

1. Thus, Eusebius of Caesarea, *Ecclesiastical History*, I.iii, especially I.iii.19. Note also that the doctrine of the threefold office had been strongly expressed among the Reformed, prior to Calvin, by Martin Bucer. It in an arguably Bucerian form, was also central to the Christology of Calvin's associate, Pierre Viret. On the history of the doctrine, see E. F. K. Müller, s.v. "Jesu Christi dreifaches Amt," in *Realencyclopädie der classischen Altertumswissenschaft* 8, col. 733–41; and note the rather derivative discussion in John Frederick Jansen, *Calvin's Doctrine of the Work of Christ* (London: James Clarke, 1956), 26–32.

2. Cf. Richard A. Muller, "The Christological Problem in the Thought of Jacobus Arminius," *Nederlands Archief voor Kerkgeschiedenis* 68 (1988): 150–52.

3. Arminius's covenantal thought is the subject of two studies, Richard A. Muller, "The Federal Motif in Seventeenth Century Arminian Theology," *Nederlands Archief voor Kerkgeschiedenis* 62, no. 1 (1982): 102–22; and Raymond A. Blacketer, "Arminius' Concept of Covenant in Its Historical Context," *Nederlands archief voor kerkgeschiedenis* 80, no. 2 (2000): 193–220, neither of which explores in any detail the interrelationship of covenantal thought with the doctrine of Christ's office. F. Stuart Clarke, *The Ground of Election: Jacob Arminius' Doctrine of the Work and Person of Christ*, Studies in Christian History and Thought (Milton Keynes, UK: Paternoster, 2006),

51–60, does address the covenantal terms used in Arminius's discussion of the priestly office but makes no attempt to explain the context of these formulations.

4. See Richard A. Muller, "Toward the *Pactum Salutis*: Locating the Origins of a Concept," *Mid-America Journal of Theology* 18 (2007): 12–13.

5. *Disp. priv.*, V.1, 3–5; cited from *Opera*, 11. Cf. Richard A. Muller, *Post-Reformation Reformed Dogmatics: The Rise and Development of Reformed Orthodoxy, ca. 1520 to ca. 1725*, 4 vols. (Grand Rapids: Baker, 2003), 1:168–70.

6. Arminius, *De sacerdotio Christi*, in *Opera*, 11; *Works*, 1:406.

7. *Disp. priv.*, XXIV.13; cf. Richard A. Muller, "God, Predestination, and the Integrity of the Created Order: A Note on Patterns in Arminius' Theology," in *Later Calvinism: International Perspectives*, ed. W. Fred Graham, Sixteenth Century Essays & Studies (Kirksville, Mo.: Sixteenth Century Journal Publishers, 1994), 431–46.

8. Arminius, *De sacerdotio Christi*, 11; *Works*, 1:406; cf. similarly, Junius, *Theses Leidenses*, XXV.6; and Franciscus Gomarus, *Disputationes theologicae*, XIII.29, in Franciscus Gomarus, *Opera theologica omnia, maximam partem posthuma* (Amsterdam: Joannes Janson, 1664), pt. 2.

9. Arminius, *De sacerdotio Christi*, 11; *Works*, 1:406.

10. Ibid.; *Works*, 1:407.

11. Ibid., 12; *Works*, 1:407–9.

12. Ibid.; *Works*, 1:409.

13. Ibid., 12–13; *Works*, 1:409.

14. Cf. Ibid., 14–15; *Works*, 1:412–15; with Arminius, *De obiecto theologiae*, in *Opera*, 34; *Works*, 1:334–335.

15. Cf. William Ames, *Rescriptio scholastica & brevis ad Nic. Grevinchovii responsum illud prolixum, quod opposuit dissertationi de redemptione generali, & electione ex fide praevisa* (Harderwijk: Nicolas à Wieringen, 1645), i (5); Herman Witsius, *De oeconomia foederum Dei cum hominibus, libri quatuor* (Leeuwarden: J. Hagenaar, 1677; second edition, 1685), II.ii.16; and see Muller, "Toward the *Pactum Salutis*," 11–65.

16. Philip van Limborch, *Theologia christiana ad praxin pietatis ac promotionem pacis christiana unice directa* (Amsterdam: Henricus Wetstenius, 1686), III.xv, xviii (243, 257); cf. Robert S. Franks, *The Work of Christ: A Historical Study of Christian Doctrine*, 2d ed. (London: Thomas Nelson, 1962), 380, 382.

17. Arminius, *De sacerdotio Christi*, 16; *Works*, 1:416.

18. Ames, *Medulla theologiae* (London: Robert Allott, 1630), I.xix.4.

19. Arminius, *De obiecto theologiae*, 34; *Works*, 1:334–35.

20. Ibid., 38; *Works*, 1:343.

21. Arminius, *De sacerdotio Christi*, 16; *Works*, 1:416–17.

22. *Disp. priv.*, XXXV.3, XXXVII.2.

23. Ibid., XXXIX.4.

24. Ibid., XXXIX.5.

25. Arminius, *De sacerdotio Christi*, 15; *Works*, 1:414.
26. Ibid., 16; *Works*, 1:415.
27. Ibid.; *Works*, 1:415–16.
28. Franciscus Gomarus, *Dispvtationvm theologicarvm decima-nona, de officio Christi: quam...præside Francisco Gomaro...publice examinandam proponit Renatvs Textor...25 Jun. 1603* (Leiden: Ioannes Patius, 1603), ii; cf. Zacharias Ursinus, *Explicationum catecheticarum, editio altera* (Cambridge: Thomas Thomasius, 1587), 366.
29. *Dec. sent.*, in *Opera*, 119; *Works*, 1:653; cf. *Disp. priv.*, XIX.6, in *Opera*, 357; *Works*, 2:245–46.
30. *Disp. pub.*, XIV.5.
31. Cf. Limborch, *Theologia Christiana*, III.xv, xvi, xvii (243, 245, 251).
32. *Disp. pub.*, XIV.6.
33. Ibid.
34. Ibid., XIV.7; cf. *Disp. priv.*, XXXVI.3.
35. *Disp. pub.*, XIV.7, citing John 1:18.
36. Ibid., cf. *Disp. priv.*, XXXVI.2.
37. Ursinus, *Explicationum catecheticarum*, 370; Franciscus Gomarus, *Disputationum theologicarum quarto repetitarum decima-nona de officiis Filii Dei incarnati...sub tutela F. Gomari...propugnare conabor Daniel Guerinellus...9 Nov. 1605* (Leiden: Ioannes Patius, 1605), vii.
38. Gomarus, *Disputationum... de officiis Filii Dei incarnati* (1605), v.
39. Gulielmus Bucanus, *Institutiones theologicae, seu locorum communium Christianae religionis, ex Dei verbo, et praestantissimorum theologorum orthodoxo consensu expositorum* (Geneva, 1602; Bern: Iohannes & Isaias Le Preux, 1605), ii.27 (23).
40. Ursinus, *Explicationum catecheticarum*, 374.
41. *Disp. priv.*, XXXV.5.
42. Ibid., XXXV.1.
43. Ibid., XIV.1.
44. Ibid., XXIV.1–2.
45. Ibid., XXXV.1.
46. Ibid., XXXV.2.
47. Ibid., XXXV.3.
48. Ibid., XXXV.5.
49. Ursinus, *Explicationum catecheticarum*, 367, 372–73.
50. Ibid., 373; Ursinus, however, does not press the issue of Melchizedek but references specifically the differences between the functions of the priesthood in general and the added functions of the high priest.
51. *Disp. pub.*, XIV.11.
52. Cf. the discussion in Richard A. Muller, *Calvin and the Reformed Tradition: Studies on the Work of Christ and the Order of Salvation* (Grand Rapids: Baker, 2012), 99–103.

53. *Disp. priv.*, XXXV.6; cf. the same structure of argument in Arminius, *De sacerdotio Christi*, 18, 20; *Works*, 1:419, 423.
54. Arminius, *De sacerdotio Christi*, 18; *Works*, 1:419–20.
55. Ibid., 19; *Works*, 1:421: "*sacrificium sufficiens tollendis omnium hominum peccatis oblatum.*"
56. Ibid.; *Works*, 1:422, citing Matt 28:18; Heb 7:17.
57. *Disp. priv.*, XXXVII.1; cf. ibid., XXXVIII.11.
58. Ibid., XXXVII.2.
59. Ibid.
60. Ibid., XXXVII.3; cf. the same division of functions or acts of office in *Disp. pub.*, XIV.19.
61. *Disp. priv.*, XXXVII.4.
62. Ibid., XXXVII.7.
63. Lucas Trelcatius Jr., *Scholastica et methodica locorum communium s. theologiae institutio, didactice & elenctice in epitome explicata: in qua, veritas locorum communium, definitionis cuiusque, loci per causas suas analysi asseritur: contraria vero argumenta, imprimis Bellarmini, generalium solutionum appendice refutantur* (London: John Bill, 1604), II.vii (75–76); Gomarus, *Dispvtationvm...de officio Christi* (1603), x–xi.

CHAPTER 2

WAS ARMINIUS AN UNWITTING DETERMINIST? ANOTHER LOOK AT ARMINIUS'S MODAL LOGIC

Thomas H. McCall

INTRODUCTION

There is much that is unclear in (most) debates over providence and predestination. What *is* reasonably clear is the fact that modality matters a lot in such discussions. What is *almost* as clear is the fact that many contemporary theologians either don't work with well-developed accounts of modality or are coy about the details of these accounts.

But it wasn't always so. In 1598, before his appointment to the professorship of theology at Leiden and the outbreak of his controversies with his colleagues there, Arminius wrote a letter to his friend Johannes Uytenbogaert in which he offers insight into his (developing) views of modal logic.[1] The content of this letter reminds us of the fact that we simply must read Arminius as a scholastic theologian if we are to understand him well, and it underscores the fact that logical and metaphysical concerns loomed large in the theological debates of the early modern era.

This letter largely has escaped the attention of Arminius scholars; perhaps this oversight reflects the lack of attention to the scholastic elements of Arminius's theology, or perhaps the predisposition of some Arminius scholars to interpret Arminius as a "biblical" (rather than scholastic) theologian works to filter out careful study of such documents. The rare exception here is the penetrating and helpful analysis offered by Eef Dekker.[2] Dekker argues that while Arminius is heavily invested in opposing (what he takes to be) the deterministic tendencies of his opponents, the surprising truth is that Arminius's own account of modality commits *him* to determinism. As he puts it, "We must conclude that Arminius himself is a *determinist*."[3]

What follows revisits Arminius's modal logic. Dekker may be correct in his analysis of this letter and its contents, but Arminius later significantly alters his views. With a bit of further correction Arminius's position can avoid determinism.

THE LETTER AND ITS ANALYSIS

Arminius lays out several logical formulae in this letter, and he applies these directly to the doctrines of providence and predestination. In addition to *possibility* and *necessity*, he is also concerned in these formulations to account for *certainty*. Using the normal modal operators ($\lozenge$ for *possibility* and $\square$ for *necessity*), letting S stand for the property being saved, D for the property being damned, and adding the operator $\mathbb{C}$ for (the still ambiguous notion of) *certainty*, we can summarize (the relevant aspects of) his views. Arminius opposes

(1) For some person x, x is saved: $(\exists x)(Sx)$

with

(2) For some person x, x is damned: $(\exists x)(Dx)$.

So far, so good; this much is noncontroversial. Once one understands what *salvation* and *damnation* mean in traditional Christian theology, it is easy to see that *being saved* and *being damned* are contradictory. No one is both saved and damned. But Arminius also opposes

(1*) For some person x, it is possible that x is saved: $(\exists x)(\Diamond Sx)$

with

(2*) For some person x, it is possible that x is not saved—that is, is damned: $(\exists x)(\Diamond Dx)$.[4]

In other words, just as he takes (1) and (2) to be contradictory, he also takes (1*) and (2*) to be contradictory.

But if (1) and (2) are contradictory (rather than contrary), then both (1) and (2) cannot be true but either (1) or (2) must be true. Accordingly, this means that necessarily, either (1*) is true and (2*) is false, or (2*) is true and (1*) is false. If (1*) is true and (2*) is false, then if x is possibly saved then it is not possible that x is not saved. Recognition of this point leads Dekker to conclude that, for Arminius,

(A) possibility and necessity are (strictly) equivalent ($\Diamond = \Box$).[5]

And (A) gives us reason, as Dekker points out, to "conclude that Arminius was a determinist."[6]

Dekker has other reasons for supposing that Arminius's modal logic commits him to determinism. He argues that Arminius's views entail the conclusion that

(B) certainty and necessity are equivalent ($\mathbb{C} = \Box$) (or, minimally, $\mathbb{C} \Rightarrow \Box$).[7]

If (B) is true then we are left with

(3) For some person x, x is *certainly* saved: $(\exists x)(\mathbb{C}Sx)$

as equivalent to

(4) For some person x, x is *necessarily* saved: $(\exists x)(\Box Sx)$.

But surely this is unpalatable to the theologian who wishes to resist determinism, for if (B) is true and (3) really is equivalent to (4) (or even implies it), then for any person whom God knows will be saved, that person will be saved of necessity. And, of course, anyone whose damnation is known by God is thus damned necessarily.

Dekker concludes that the endorsement of (A) and (B) make

(C) *Either* one is saved, and necessarily so, and is certain of this, *or* one is not saved, and necessarily so, and is certain of one's being not saved

unavoidable for Arminius. Dekker's pronouncement is surely grim (for any opponent of theological determinism): "In this law determinism is present once more. Right at the point at which Arminius attacks his Calvinist fellow theologians, he turns out to be guilty himself. In (C) there is a determinist logic of predestination."[8]

ARMINIUS'S CHANGES

Dekker correctly maintains that the formulations offered by Arminius in this letter are not quite satisfactory. If this were all that Arminius had said, we might reasonably conclude that Arminius was an unwitting determinist (as well, perhaps, as hopelessly confused). But this is *not* all that Arminius said, for he later offers us further reflections upon modality.[9] For instance, in his *Examen thesium D. Francisci Gomari de praedestinatione* he gives additional insights into his views.[10] With respect to

(A) possibility and necessity are (strictly) equivalent

he clearly distinguishes between necessity and contingency, and he says that "such things as these cannot coincide." Necessity and contingency, he insists, are "contradictory," for "that which cannot *not* be done (*non potest non fieri*), comes to pass necessarily; and that which can *not* be done (*potest non fieri*), comes to pass contingently: but to be able not to be done (*posse autem non fieri*), and *not* to be able not to be done (*non posse non fieri*), are contradictory terms."[11] Moreover, Arminius plainly opposes possibility and necessity; what "can happen" is actually *contradictory* (rather than merely contrary) to what "cannot not-happen."[12] Far from being equivalent, they are contradictory—both cannot be true, but one must be true.

As we have seen in his letter to Uytenbogaert, Arminius makes claims that entail

(B) certainty and necessity are equivalent

But by the time of his controversial engagement with Gomarus, he clearly distinguishes between certainty and necessity. He explains that certainty pertains to epistemology rather than to the metaphysics of modality. Necessity, on the other hand, is a modal property.

> *Certainty* properly is not an affection of an existing thing or of one about to happen, but of the mind certainly knowing or foreknowing that the thing exists or is about to exist: whence a transference is made to the event of the thing; not that any mode is added to the event—for it is the same thing that a thing will happen, and that it will *certainly* happen.... But *necessity* is an affection of being (*affectus entis*), and adds a mode to the event, by which it is said that a thing will happen *necessarily*, and is opposed to the mode which is called contingency.[13]

Thus "the same idea is not expressed, when it is said that a thing will happen *certainly* and *necessarily*, for the one word is only about futurition, the other about the mode also of futurition."[14] So for Arminius, at least by the time of his engagement with Gomarus, certainty is *not* to be equated with necessity. Nor does certainty entail necessity. To the contrary, Arminius is convinced that the confusion of certainty with necessity results in a lot of theological mischief.[15]

As we have seen, Dekker makes a strong case that Arminius (in the letter under consideration) is committed to (A) and (B) and thus—much to our surprise and likely his as well—is saddled with

(C) *Either* one is saved, and necessarily so, and is certain of this, *or* one is not saved, and necessarily so, and is certain of one's being not saved.

But as I have shown, there is good reason to think that Arminius had corrected these earlier musings (at least by the time of his controversy with Gomarus) and had disavowed both (A) and (B). Accordingly, he need not be bothered by (C).

Further Analysis: A Remaining Problem and a Suggested Remedy

By my lights, Arminius is right to make these corrective moves. With respect to (A), Arminius's letter offers no *reasons* to think that possibility and necessity are equivalent. He does not make strong *arguments* that this is the way we should think about such matters; instead he merely floats some ideas in front of a trusted friend and ally. Thus he has nothing to recant; he has no arguments of his own for that conclusion that now stare him in the face. What we have in the letter are simply his musings on modality. Whatever has happened between the writing of this letter and his engagement with Gomarus, it is clear that he now takes a different view of (A). But not all is yet bright and beautiful, for his formulations in *Exam. Gom.* are not quite free from problems. He is right to see necessity and contingency as opposed, but—alas—he also opposes necessity and possibility as contradictory. This can be seen in his square of modal opposition:[16]

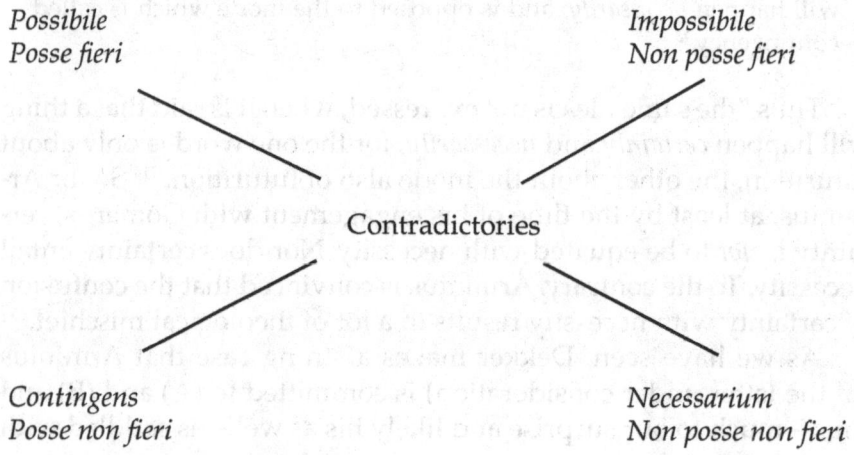

The problem, however, is that necessity is not contradictory to possibility; rather necessity subimplies possibility. In other words, if something is necessary surely it is possible—although if something is possible it need not be necessary (it could be contingent). This may be illustrated as follows:[17]

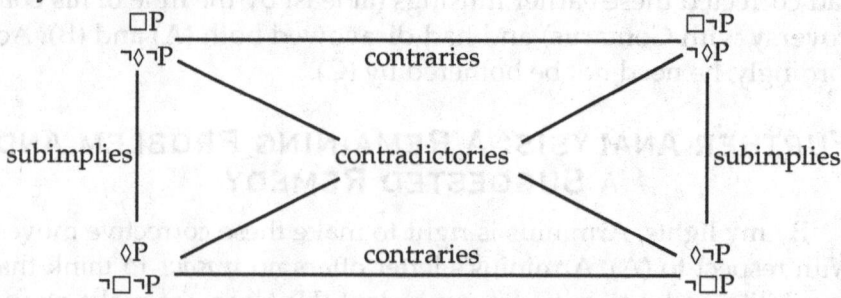

So Arminius has overcorrected, and his position seems plainly wrong. But this remaining problem is not insurmountable, and at any rate it is not fatal. There is nothing here to pull Arminius back into determinism, and all that remains for fellow Arminians on this score is to make the needed corrections.

So, Arminius is right to make these moves. With them, his view can hold to the following:

(5) Possibly, for some person x, x is saved: $\lozenge(\exists x)(Sx)$;

(6) Possibly, for some person x, x is saved and x is certainly saved: $\lozenge(\exists x)(Sx \& (\mathbb{C}Sx))$;

(7) Possibly, for some person x, x is saved and x is possibly dammed: $\lozenge(\exists x)(Sx \& (\lozenge Dx))$;

(8) Possibly, for some person x, x is saved and x is certainly saved and x is possibly damned: $\lozenge(\exists x)(Sx \& (x\mathbb{C}S) \& (\lozenge Dx))$.

This is, it seems to me, what Arminius needs for his doctrine of predestination.[18]

CERTAINTY AND NECESSITY AGAIN

But perhaps this is all too quick. Maybe Arminius would have been right initially to confuse certainty with necessity (or at least to think that necessity is entailed by certainty). Many contemporary theologians seem to think that divine foreknowledge entails determinism. As a common argument goes, the problem here—if indeed there is one—goes farther and deeper than is often recognized. But actually there really is not a problem at all.

A Common Argument

A common argument (CA) to the conclusion that divine foreknowledge is incompatible with human freedom proceeds along these fairly predictable lines:

(9) If at some time, t1, God knows what Tom will do at some later time, t2, then Tom is not free with respect to what he does at t2;[19]

(10) If God is omniscient, then God knows at t1 what Tom will do at t2;

(11) God is omniscient;

(12) Therefore, God knows at t1 what Tom will do at t2 (from 9, 10);

(13) Therefore, Tom is not free with respect to what he does at t2 (from 9, 12).[20]

The lesson most commonly learned from this familiar argument is that libertarian human freedom is not possible if God has exhaustive foreknowledge. The (CA) is most often wielded against traditional views that affirm both freedom and omniscience, but it has far-reaching implications. Here is why: The common argument can easily—and reasonably—be amended to show that it impacts *divine* freedom as well as human freedom.[21]

(9*) If at t1 God knows what God will do at t2, then God is not free with respect to what he does at t2;

(10*) If God is omniscient, then God knows at t1 what God will do at t2;

(11) God is omniscient;

(12*) Therefore, God knows at t1 what God will do at t2 (from 10*, 11);

(13*) Therefore, God is not free with respect to what he does at t2 (from 9*, 12*).[22]

Richard Swinburne sees this problem clearly, and he simply bites the metaphysical bullet. With characteristic clarity, he concludes that it is not possible for there to be a perfectly free person who is also omniscient (in the traditional sense of omniscience). And since God *is* a perfectly free person, the conclusion to be drawn is that God can "not have knowledge of his future free actions."[23] Thus God "will not know in advance what he will do."[24] Swinburne recognizes that this places a "much larger limit on God's omniscience than the limit concerned with future human free actions."[25] Swinburne does allow that there are (or may be) *some* cases where perfect goodness may constrain God to act in an "unfree" way, but other than these rare exceptions, God must necessarily be ignorant of his own future actions. As he puts it,

If God's omniscience is to include foreknowledge of his future actions, there would seem no reason to confine that foreknowledge merely to foreknowledge of some such actions; and if it included all God's future actions, he would have no freedom left. If at any time God does have perfect freedom, then always prior to that God will have been ignorant of how he will act.[26]

The result is that God's "ignorance of the future must be vast" if God is free.

If the (CA) and its less common cousin are successful, I think that there are serious problems here both for those theologians who accept this argument and deny that God has foreknowledge of God's own actions (thoroughgoing open theists) and for those theologians who accept this argument and conclude that all divine actions must be determined too. Several streams of thought in the broadly "Reformed" tradition flow in this latter direction. Especially notable are those associated with Jonathan Edwards as well as those that run through Schleiermacher and Hegel to Bruce L. McCormack's Barth-inspired proposal.[27] Yet the open theists who come to this conclusion will not be able to say nearly as much as they (typically) want to say about divine providence, and the determinists are faced with both metaphysical problems (modal collapse) and doctrinal difficulties (divine sovereignty and aseity are replaced with fatalism and monism). But such conclusions do not concern us at this point but instead the objection itself.

Not Obviously True

Is the Common Argument successful? Arminius thinks not, and he draws upon the venerable distinction between the necessity of the consequent and the necessity of the consequence.[28] Where the necessity of the consequent gives us

(14) Necessarily, if x is saved then necessarily x is not damned: $\Box\ (Sx => \Box\ \sim Dx)$

the necessity of the consequence holds only that

(15) Necessarily, if x is saved then x is not damned: $\Box\ (Sx => \sim Dx)$.

In other words, where (14) is deterministic, the necessity of (15) is completely consistent with contingency and freedom. But,

Arminius argues, there is no reason to think that the doctrine of predestination requires (14) rather than (15).

Arminius's employment of the tradition here is insightful and points to a way forward. A full exploration of this question surely is far beyond the reach of this paper but there is space to summarize three important principles that relieve much of the pressure of the Common Argument. Some insights that build upon the foundation laid in the kind of approach that Arminius takes (and that are commonly associated with "Ockham's Way Out") call (9) into question.[29]

First, we should remember that *knowledge is not causal*. The Common Argument does not advance the claim that knowledge *is* causal nor is there good reason to suppose that it should. One's knowledge of a current event does not make it true; the very fact that from a distance one observes an accident does not mean that one caused the accident to happen. Nor, for that matter, does one's knowledge of past events in any way cause them to occur. Similarly, foreknowledge of a future event does not cause the occurrence of the event, and a prophet who is given insight into future events might truly be said to know these things without this knowledge causing them to occur. We have no good reasons to think that knowledge is causal but plenty of reasons to think that it is not.

The second principle is that *the modal status of a proposition does not change*.[30] To see this, consider the proposition *Tom sets the ringtone of the phone of a senior colleague to Right Said Fred's "I'm Too Sexy" on 8 December 2013*. This proposition is logically contingent. As such, it is logically contingent in 2013. It was also contingent when Nero burned Rome, and for that matter, when the camp cook burned the bacon in 2013. It will be contingent in 3013, just as it is now. As Keith Yandell puts it, "Whatever modal status a proposition enjoyed yesterday, it has now. Any proposition of the form *Person X freely does A at time t* is logically contingent. So it is *always* logically contingent—at t, before t, and after t."[31] To say this is not to deny accidental necessity (or the "necessity of the consequence"), but accidental necessity is not incompatible with logical contingency.

The third truth to keep in mind is that the direction of entailment is not the same thing as the direction of truth determination. If I freely prank a senior theologian by setting his ringtone to Right Said Fred's "I'm Too Sexy" (and then calling him while he is in, say, a prayer meeting), then (if God is omniscient, at least omniscient in the classical sense) God knows that I will do so. And, if God knows that I will do it, then surely I will do it. So, entailment runs both ways, from God's knowledge of something to the action itself and from the action itself to God's knowledge of it. But this is not the same thing as the direction of truth determination. As we have seen, the knowledge itself is not causal. So what *does* make such a statement true? Well, a prime candidate for this honor is *what happens on 8 December 2013*. That is, whether or not the proposition is true depends on what Tom *does* on 8 December 2013.[32]

With these principles in mind, we see that the alleged problem is not quite so serious as is usually supposed. Of course we are left with many questions. What "grounds" these counterfactuals of freedom?[33] Is "Ockham's Way Out" compatible with divine temporality, or does it require a view of God as atemporal?[34] And *how* does God know the future?[35] I have not begun to address such questions as these, and they are important. Still, we should be able to see—even from this brief sketch—why the Common Argument may not be so worrisome as is often supposed. As Yandell puts it, "While the direction of entailment is mutual, the direction of truth-determination is one-way, and it is one-way in a manner that prevents the alleged problem from arising."[36] We can affirm God's knowledge of future events, including robustly free human choices to accept or reject the grace of God, without also stepping into determinism.

CONCLUSION

So, was Arminius a determinist—albeit an unwitting one? The clear answer is that he was *not*. Dekker's work is extremely insightful and helpful. The modal logic offered to Uytenbogaert may indeed not be sufficient for the doctrinal work at hand. We need, however, to keep several things in mind. First, this letter merely explores these possibilities. Second, Arminius floats these ideas to a friend with obvious tentativeness.[37] Third, and more important, his later work avoids these problems.[38]

So (once again) was Arminius a determinist? In the narrow sense that he says things *in this letter* that appear to leave him unable to escape determinism, the answer might be yes. In the broader sense of Arminius's own intentions, clearly not. And in the broader sense of his corpus and legacy, the answer should be as clear as his own intentions: Arminius is *not* committed to determinism, either intentionally or unintentionally. He strives mightily to overcome it, and his mature work contains the resources necessary to do so.

NOTES

1. Published as No. 57 in *Praestantium ac eruditorum virorum epistolae ecclesiasticae et theologicae*, ed. Philip von Limborch and Christian Hartsoecker (Amsterdam: H. Wetstenium, 1684), 57–61.

2. Eef Dekker, "Jacob Arminius and His Logic: Analysis of a Letter," *Journal of Theological Studies* 44 (1993): 118–42. Dekker notes that Carl Bangs translates part of this letter as well, cf. C. Bangs, 203–5.

3. Dekker, "Jacob Arminius and His Logic," 126.

4. E.g., Arminius, in *Praestantium ac eruditorum virorum epistolae ecclesiasticae et theologicae*, 57; Dekker, "Jacob Arminius and His Logic," 139. Arminius does much more here as well, but the present examples suffice.

5. Dekker, "Jacob Arminius and His Logic," 126.

6. Ibid.

7. Ibid., 127.

8. Ibid., 128. He thinks that the most that Arminius does to mitigate this determinism is to introduce "a kind of epistemological indeterminism on the human side," but he thinks that this move "does not loosen the ties of metaphysical determinism and leads to further incoherences" (ibid., 138).

9. Questions about the transition of his own views (questions about the extent to which he changed his views, the intentionality with which he changed his views, or the possible influences upon him that impacted these changes) are beyond the scope of this essay.

10. *Exam. Gom.* This is a helpful treatise because it is written later, and in the midst of the controversies over predestination. An English translation is available in *Works*, 3:521–658.

11. Ibid., 32; *Works*, 3:552.

12. Ibid.; *Works*, 3:553.

13. Ibid., 25; *Works*, 3:547.

14. Ibid., 25–26; *Works*, 3:547.

15. These discussions are hampered by ambiguity regarding the meaning of "certainty." It may be taken in the rather tautologous sense (C_i), where "certainly will happen" is just equivalent to "really will happen" or just "will happen"; it may be taken in the sense of (C_{ii}), the certainty of divine knowledge; and it may also be taken in the sense of (C_{iii}), the certainty of the human person as a kind of psychological certainty. Dekker works with (C_{iii}), but by the time of his engagement with Gomarus, it is clear that Arminius is working with the sense of (C_i). For

discussion of these issues in medieval scholasticism, see, e.g., A. Vos, "Knowledge, Certainty, and Contingency," in *John Duns Scotus: The Renewal of Philosophy*, ed. E. P. Bos (Amsterdam: Rodopi, 1994), 75–88.

16. *Exam. Gom.*, 32; *Works*, 3:553.

17. William Lane Craig and J. P. Moreland, *Philosophical Foundations for a Christian Worldview* (Downers Grove, Ill.: InterVarsity Press, 2003), 49.

18. This is not, of course, *all* that Arminius needs for his doctrine of predestination. Nor is it obviously enough to separate it from all Reformed accounts. But it is enough to escape the charge of metaphysical determinism.

19. This formulation proceeds with a "temporalist" view of God and time, because most proponents of (CA) make this assumption, and it is easier to state the objection in this way.

20. This particular formulation of the familiar problem follows that of Keith E. Yandell, *Philosophy of Religion: A Contemporary Introduction* (New York: Routledge, 1999), 335.

21. Issues related to divine freedom are notoriously complex (especially as they relate to divine goodness and perfection). On these see William L. Rowe, *Can God Be Free?* (Oxford: Oxford University Press, 2004). My own view is that there may be any number of galaxies of possible worlds that are feasible for God (where God is understood as perfectly good) and that God is at liberty to choose between and among these. For arguments here see Thomas P. Flint and Alfred J. Freddoso, "Maximal Power," in *The Concept of God*, ed. Thomas V. Morris (Oxford: Oxford University Press, 1987), 134–67; and Thomas P. Flint, "The Problem of Divine Freedom," *American Philosophical Quarterly* (1983): 255–64. For a direct (and helpful) response to Rowe, see Thomas D. Senor, "Defending Divine Freedom," in *Oxford Studies in Philosophy of Religion*, vol. 1, ed. Jonathan L. Kvanvig (Oxford: Oxford University Press, 2008), 168–95. Edward Wierenga sounds a cautionary note here; he thinks that divine freedom and action are so different from human action as to call into question straightforward ascriptions of various notions of freedom to God; see Wierenga, "The Freedom of God," *Faith and Philosophy* (2002): 425–36.

22. This argument can be found among the oft-overlooked Methodist theologians of the nineteenth century; e.g., Thomas N. Ralston, *Elements of Divinity* (Nashville: Southern Methodist Publishing House, 1871), 182; Samuel Wakefield, *A Complete System of Christian Theology* (Cincinnati: Cranston and Stowe, 1869), 334–35.

23. Richard Swinburne, *The Coherence of Theism*, rev. ed. (Oxford: Oxford University Press, 1993), 179.

24. Ibid., 181.

25. Richard Swinburne, *The Christian God* (Oxford: Oxford University Press, 1994), 134.

26. Ibid.

27. E.g., Bruce L. McCormack, "Grace and Being: The Role of God's Gracious Election in Karl Barth's Theological Ontology," in *The Cambridge Companion to Karl Barth*, ed. John Webster (Cambridge: Cambridge University Press, 2000), 92–110; and Micheal T. Dempsey, ed., *Trinity and Election in Contemporary Theology* (Grand Rapids: Eerdmans, 2011). In many important ways, Arminius and his Reformed opponents have more in common with each other than either has with "Reformed" theologies that espouse divine determinism. Cf. Willem J. Van Asselt, J. Martin Bac, and Roelf T. te Velde, eds., *Reformed Thought on Freedom: The Concept of Free Choice in Early Modern Reformed Theology* (Grand Rapids: Baker Academic, 2010).

28. E.g., *Exam. Gom.*, 28; *Works*, 3:549.

29. Alvin Plantinga, "On Ockham's Way Out," *Faith and Philosophy* 3 (1986): 235–69. Much of this particular formulation is indebted to Keith Yandell.

30. The system of modal logic known as S5 supports this claim; the important axiom here is $\Diamond P \Rightarrow \exists \Diamond P$. On the place of S5 in the development of systems of modal logic, see Michael J. Loux, "Introduction: Modality and Metaphysics," in *The Possible and the Actual: Readings in the Metaphysics of Modality*, ed. Michael J. Loux (Ithaca: Cornell University Press, 1979), 15–64.

31. Keith E. Yandell, *The Epistemology of Religious Experience* (Cambridge: Cambridge University Press, 1993), 360.

32. This may raise the question of retrocausation: Does what I say entail that we have causal power over the past? No, for all we have is counterfactual control over God's beliefs, not causal control. On this see William Lane Craig, "Divine Foreknowledge and Newcomb's Paradox," *Philosophia* 17 (1987): 331–50.

33. William Lane Craig argues forcefully that the so-called "Grounding Objection" has not yet been clearly stated. See especially his "Middle Knowledge, Truth-Makers, and the Grounding Objection," *Faith and Philosophy* (2001): 337–52.

34. Michael C. Rea and Alicia Finch argue that the Ockhamist strategy requires Eternalism; see their "Presentism and Ockham's Way Out," in Kvanvig, *Oxford Studies in Philosophy of Religion*, 1–17.

35. On this see Alvin Plantinga, "Divine Knowledge," in *Christian Perspectives on Religious Knowledge*, ed. C. Stephen Evans and Merold Westphal (Grand Rapids: Eerdmans, 1993), 40–65. For discussion of the issue in late medieval scholasticism, see, e.g., Eef Dekker, "Does Duns Scotus Need Molina? On Divine Foreknowledge and Co-causality," in *John Duns Scotus: Renewal of Philosophy*, 113–22; and Gloria Frost, "John Duns

Scotus on God's Knowledge of Sins: A Test-Case for God's Knowledge of Contingents," *Journal of the History of Philosophy* (2010): 15–34.

36. Yandell, *The Epistemology of Religious Experience*, 361.

37. E.g., Dekker, "Jacob Arminius and His Logic," 138, 142.

38. This is true whether or not, or to what extent, Arminius *realized* that these were problems.

CHAPTER 3

BEYOND LUTHER, BEYOND CALVIN, BEYOND ARMINIUS: THE PILGRIMS AND THE REMONSTRANTS IN LEIDEN, 1609–1620

Jeremy Dupertuis Bangs

Before the Pilgrims undertook their famous 1620 voyage to America on the *Mayflower*, their exile in Leiden since 1609 placed them in the midst of the great conflicts between the followers of Jacob Arminius and those of Francis Gomarus, the Remonstrants and the Contra-Remonstrants. The Pilgrims' minister John Robinson was drawn into the theological turmoil. When the first Pilgrims departed for New England, Robinson bewailed

> the state and condition of the Reformed Churches, who were come to a period in Religion, and would go no further than the instruments of their Reformation. As for example the Lutherans, they could not be drawn to go beyond what Luther saw, for whatever part of God's will he had further imparted and revealed to Calvin, they will rather die than embrace it. And so also...the Calvinists, they stick where he left them.[1]

Nor should Robinson's own followers idolize what he had taught them, but, "if God should reveal anything...by any other instrument of his, [they should] be as ready to receive it."[2] Robinson was confident that "the Lord had more truth and light yet to break forth out of his holy Word."

What then was the "state and condition of the Reformed Churches" when the Pilgrims lived in Leiden? What provoked intervention by King James I of England? What role did John Robinson play? What new truth and light was breaking forth? These questions will concern us here.[3]

1603–1608: James I, John Robinson, and the Birth of the Pilgrims

The Pilgrims originated in England's Puritan movement of the sixteenth century. When Queen Elizabeth I died and was succeeded by her cousin King James VI of Scotland (who became James I of England), many Puritans hoped for further reformation in the direction of Scottish Presbyterianism. Among the hopeful Reformists, John Robinson, a former dean of Corpus Christi College in Cambridge and the future minister of the Pilgrims, even preached a sermon thanking God "for sending him [King James] to reign over us, by whose reign there is great hope of the continuance of peace and the gospel to be preached."[4]

Dire warnings accompanied this fervent hope. For, Robinson continued, if the English did not "turn to the Lord and repent," God would punish the land by taking "away their prince and king from them." Threatening God's vengeance was commonplace. Tension arose from the confrontation of the demand for individual moral choice with the question of the definition and extent of God's knowledge of, and consequent responsibility for, the future—predestination. Robinson had learned the assumptions of this sort of theology when he studied at Cambridge under the renowned Calvinist theologian William Perkins. (Arminius's posthumously published "Examination of Perkins' Pamphlet" contradicts not only Perkins but also beliefs held by Robinson.[5])

In a dramatic confrontation with the new king in 1603, ministers claiming to represent over a thousand dissatisfied Puritans demanded major reforms. The king heard their complaints the next year at Hampton Court Palace but ultimately refused to carry out more than a few minor changes. Robinson lost his enthusiasm for King James when the monarch commented that the issues that mattered most to the Puritans were not of prime importance and should be left to academic discussion. The Puritans' protest provoked the famous royal threat, "If this be all that they have to say, I shall make them conform themselves, or I will harry them out of the land, or else do worse."[6] New rules required conformity.

Yet shortly after the Hampton Court Conference, Robinson was moved by two sermons he heard in Cambridge to question conforming to the Church of England.[7] First, Lawrence Chadderton preached on the text "Tell it to the Church" (Matt 18:17) and championed this as a divine command that all major problems be discussed before the entire congregation. Robinson observed that this practice was followed nowhere in the Church of England in dealing with censure. Instead, sinners were summoned before church courts external to their own congregations. For Robinson this raised an all-important question. How could he, knowing what a church should be, remain a member of an impure church, the Church of England?

In the afternoon William Perkins's successor, Paul Baynes, preached on the Christian's obligation to withdraw from association with the ungodly, or as Robinson put it, "the unlawfulness of familiar conversation between the servants of God, & the wicked." Had not God separated the light from the darkness? Would not outsiders be offended, Robinson asked himself, "and occasioned to think them all alike, and as birds of a feather which so flock together?"[8] The conclusion was clear. God had separated the light from the darkness, so that meant the godly should withdraw from the unconverted. This was a turning point in Robinson's life. Rather than feeling his heart strangely warmed, Robinson's mind was gripped by the cold clarity of Calvinist logic.

In 1606, Robinson joined other Puritan theologians to decide their response to the newly imposed rules requiring conformity; among the others attending were John Dod, Arthur Hildersam, Richard Clyfton, John Smyth, and Richard Bernard. Some opted to remain quietly in the Church of England; these included Dod and Hildersham. Up until this meeting, Clyfton and Bernard apparently still thought local congregations might be reformed by the creation of covenanted small groups within them (*ecclesiolæ in ecclesiæ*—the form of the later Pietist movement or perhaps prototypical home groups). Smyth and Robinson argued for separation, evidently convincing Clyfton.

While Robinson swayed Clyfton, it was Clyfton who stood at the geographic center of the birth of the Pilgrims. Robinson at this time still lived in Norwich, where he was ejected from his position as assistant minister at St. Andrew's. Clyfton had been deprived of his position as rector of Babworth in 1605. He became the first minister of the Separatist congregation that formed at Scrooby in 1606 and later became known as the Pilgrims. Even while rector of Babworth, Clyfton was preaching alternately in the nearby churches of Bawtry and Scrooby, whose Puritan laymen supported this ministry financially.

Chief among these laymen was William Brewster. Brewster had studied at Cambridge. He left to become the personal secretary of William Davison, a government official who became England's secretary of state. Brewster also accompanied Davison on a diplomatic visit to the Netherlands in 1585-1586. Among the cities visited was Leiden. Brewster, having acquired an unusually broad acquaintance with international politics, returned around 1595 to his boyhood home of Scrooby. He succeeded his father as postmaster and manager of Scrooby Manor, owned by the Archbishop of York.

In 1598, Brewster was charged with "repeating sermons publicly in the church without authority."[9] In other words, Brewster had been leading dissenting religious discussions in the parish church before finally becoming one of the leaders of the separated group covenanted together in 1606, which met secretly in the manor house and sometimes elsewhere. John Robinson joined this group on returning to the home of his youth in nearby Sturton-le-Steeple sometime in the spring or summer of 1607. The Separatists in this area grew and formed two distinct congregations. Besides Scrooby, another focus was Gainsborough, where John Smyth was the preacher and Thomas Helwys one of the leading laymen. (Helwys later became a founder of the English Baptist Church.)

Increasing pursuit forced these believers to meet in secret. That Brewster and Helwys lived in moated manor houses gave some security, as did the support of Thomas Hickman of Gainsborough Old Hall. People who stayed away from the parish church on Sunday were hauled before the ecclesiastical courts and fined. Presentments and reprimands, excommunications and reinstatements, these were just the beginnings of increasing penalties. This well-known sequence included severe fines, imprisonment, and, in cases of intransigence, automatic sentence of confiscation of property and banishment out of the country. The persecution was remembered years later. They "were hunted and persecuted on every side, so as their former afflictions were but as flea-bitings in comparison. For some were taken & clapped up in prison, others had their houses beset & watched night and day, & hardly escaped."[10]

On January 20, 1607, a tsunami hit the southwest of England, with huge waves rushing up the Bristol Channel, flooding fourteen miles inland and submerging more than thirty villages in England and Wales. People were sure this was the punishing hand of God; a pamphlet called it *God's Warning to His people of England*.[11] The tsunami was followed by drought, harvest failure, and famine. At the end of summer, word arrived in the Scrooby area that the plague had returned to London and other cities. Scrooby had felt the plague already in 1602 and 1603. Now death had returned. Finally, beginning in mid-September, a spectacular comet appeared in the western sky—surely a sign of God's displeasure.

Divine portents pointed Robinson and his coreligionists elsewhere. The Pilgrims rapidly took measures to flee to the Netherlands where they knew that other Separatists had enjoyed religious freedom since the 1590s. They felt compelled to create a true church. After nine months in Amsterdam, most of them moved to Leiden.

1609: ARMINIUS AND ROBINSON AS NEIGHBORS IN LEIDEN

In Leiden, among thousands of other refugees, the Pilgrims found places to live where they could. Indeed, at this time, refugees accounted for a third of Leiden's population of ca. 45,000. William Brewster rented a house behind the great Pieterskerk. John Robinson lived on one side of the square in front of the church, becoming a neighbor of Arminius, whose house also faced the churchyard. Arminius's opponent Francis Gomarus lived at the end of the street where Robinson lived, just beyond the university building across the bridge. Leiden is a small town. People know each other. Robinson and Arminius very likely met, even though Arminius was ill and died about six months after the Pilgrims arrived.

FRANCISCUS GOMARUS THEOLOGIÆ PRIMARIUS PROFESSOR.

Arminus's neighbor and chief theological advisary, Francis Gomarus. Courtesy of The Leiden American Pilgrim Museum.

The public conflicts between Arminius and Gomarus had attracted public attention since their appearance before the States of Holland (i.e., the governing assembly of the province of Holland) in the summer of 1608. Robinson was not, however, immediately enrolled in these disputes. He gave his attention to answering (in print) objections to separation raised by old friends from England who did not become Separatists: John Burgess, Joseph Hall, and Richard Bernard.

From his residence in Leiden, Robinson responded to his critics in England by composing his book *Justification of Separation* (published in 1610).[12] In terms of method and logic, Robinson and Arminius were quite close. Like many others of the time, they used the Bible as a uniform field of terms that needed to be combined in acceptably logical demonstrations. They were not only common practitioners of scholastic theology in a general sense but even owed a common debt to the particular theories and methods of Jacomo Zabarella (1533–1589).

For Zabarella, two methods led to truth. Composition, the method of metaphysics, including theology, is a demonstrative argument from general principles to particular effects. Resolution, the method of the practical rather than contemplative sciences, proceeds from particular effects back to the general principles they exemplify. When the syllogisms of the two methods (deductive and inductive) produce identical conclusions (although in reverse order), they provide mutual confirmation.[13]

Zabarella's version captivated the attention of Protestant Scholastics in the late sixteenth century and early seventeenth centuries in northern Europe. After all, they were seeking a way to test Scripture against Scripture in order to determine the right interpretation without dependence on papal authority and Catholic tradition. Arminius had travelled to Padua expressly to hear Zabarella lecture. In his letter to John Burgess in 1609, Robinson explicitly referred to Zabarella as the source of philosophical distinctions that supported Robinson's definition of the words *church* and *churches* as referring to "particular assemblies & spiritual societies."[14] Their respective theologies were not without affinities, either. For example, like Calvin and classical Christian theologians indebted to Plato's philosophy, Arminius staunchly maintained the traditional divine attributes, including the immutability of God.

The relationship of Scripture, tradition, and the formulation of doctrine was more complicated for Arminius and Robinson, but there are some affinities between the two figures. Arminius insisted often on the vital necessity of humility in matters of theological discussion and debate. While some doctrines were clear and binding in the Scriptures, other matters were less than clear and invited, even demanded, a capacity to disagree agreeably. Arminius maintained a positive role for tradition, including church councils, as witnesses to the divine truth of the Bible. Councils could err, but they did not necessarily err. John Robinson had a more radical sense of the provisionality of doctrine and expressed complete mistrust in anything but the Bible (and the Apostles' Creed) as a trustworthy source of divine truth. As he wrote to his followers, "The first thing that we are to believe [is] that we must believe nothing but according to [the Holy Scriptures]. All things else are human; and human it is to err, and be deceived. The custom of the Church is but the custom of men; the sentence of the fathers but the opinion of men. The determinations of councils are but the judgements of men."[15]

That last sentiment Robinson acknowledges as coming from William Whitaker, who wrote, "Finally, councils, fathers, popes, are men; and scripture testifies that all men are deceitful."[16] This mistrust of conciliar symbols underlies the Plymouth colonists' refusal to make the Belgic Confession binding, even when their London investors demanded a formal requirement of assent by the colonists.[17] That Plymouth decision must have been inspired by the ongoing influence of Robinson's theological admonition. This radical sense of doctrinal provisionality went together with Robinson's humility in recognizing the Scripture as untamed and untamable as the source of theology.

While Arminius did maintain Whitaker's point that a faithful layperson may be an abler interpreter of the Bible than the pope, he also stressed that the truth of the Bible, conveyed in its original languages, is uniquely accessible to scholars trained in those languages. Arminius also maintained the importance of the able use of logic and syllogisms, but such methods could not stand on their own. In other words, the linguistic skills of humanist professors (such as Arminius himself) were essential to the practice of faithful biblical translation and interpretation. Robinson, on the other hand, stressed that the interpretation of the Bible, called prophesying, could be carried out by anyone, not just by the trained clergy. The key to the veracity of the interpretation was whether it could withstand critical scrutiny in its logical structure. Thus, Robinson's congregation practiced a more democratic form of religious discussion. Laymen interpreted the Scriptures, with Pastor Robinson and Elder Brewster (both university trained scholars) providing well-practiced, corrective instruction in logic.

If we assume that Robinson must have been a charismatic leader in order to inspire his church to such courageous actions as they carried out, then here must be part of the excitement. Truth could be found in the Bible by everyone, and it could be known to be true by means of the very rational, logical analysis that Robinson could provide. Not everyone had the gift of prophecy, so not all amateur commentary was equally instructive. Nonetheless, Robinson emphasized that interpreting the Bible was not a skill restricted to the clergy and that among the laymen of any proper congregation it should be expected that some could be found whose words should be heard. In fact, Robinson even points to specific examples of women with the gift of prophecy to find a general rule that at times women should legitimately speak to the church in contrast to the particular contradictory instance when the apostle Paul wanted women to be silent.

Among their theological differences, the most trenchant pertain to God's role in the fall of humanity. Arminius had objected to Perkins's theory (shared by Robinson), according to which Adam's fall was foreordained by God as a means to demonstrate mercy and justice. Arminius commented that "that sentiment is in antagonism to the justice of God as making God the author of sin, and inferring the inevitable necessity of sin.... For, allowing such a decree, it would be impossible for man to abstain from the act of sin."[18] Robinson did not expressly deny the charge that this system made God the author of sin. Rather, when repeatedly confronted with the problem of evil, Robinson maintained that evil itself must be essentially good in a superior way that imperfect men are too ignorant to understand. No doubt Robinson sought to include Isaiah 45:7, according to which (in the Geneva translation of the Bible) God said, "I forme the light and create darkeness: I make peace, and create euill: I the Lord doe all these things." Any theology that incorporated freedom of choice (and thus placed responsibility for evil on the choice of the actor) was considered a heretical attack on the divine property of omnipotent omniscience. This kind of conundrum made the imperfection of human understanding an essential aspect of Robinson's and the other Pilgrims' understanding of themselves and humanity in general.

1609–1613: ENGLISH PROTESTS TO ARMINIUS'S SUCCESSOR AT LEIDEN

While John Robinson was debating with his English acquaintances, he and the other Pilgrims settled into their life in exile. Robinson and Brewster met and became friends with some of their new neighbors, including Reformed clergy involved in the ongoing disputes that had not stopped when Arminius died in late 1609. Robinson became a member of the university and was invited to participate in the theological debates between the Arminians and the anti-Arminians. According to the chronicler of the Pilgrims, William Bradford, John Robinson was "terrible to the Arminians."[19] The three most important topics were predestination, freedom of theological debate, and the appropriate relation of church and state.

Circumstances in Holland changed rapidly after Arminius died. Johannes Uytenbogaert led the defense of Arminian views. Uytenbogaert was court preacher in The Hague and chaplain to Prince Maurits, the successor of his father Prince William the Silent as military leader of the Dutch revolt. Having consulted first with Johan van Oldenbarnevelt (who was essentially the head of Holland's civil government) in January 1610, Uytenbogaert and forty-five other Arminian clergy presented a "Remonstrance" to the provincial parliament, the States of Holland and West Friesland. They wanted continued toleration within the Reformed Church of the Arminian theological position; and they insisted that this toleration be maintained and protected by a benevolent civil authority. The Remonstrant (Arminian) position on predestination was that God, before the creation of the world, had decided to save to eternal life those who through divine grace believed in Christ and persisted in that belief until death. Such grace was not irresistible. Christ had died for all people, although only those who believed would be beneficiaries. A believer could lapse again to unbelief.

Their opponents, the Gomarists, were strict Calvinists who believed that God had predetermined, before creation, to save specific people (the "elect") and condemn specific other people (the "reprobate"). The anti-Arminians set out their ideas with a "Contra-Remonstrance." Robinson concurred with the Calvinist/Gomarist formulation of limited atonement: "The apostle's meaning, therefore, is not that Christ died for all particulars, but that all for whom he died, shall be saved by him; which seeing all are not, it followeth that he died not for all, as they [the Arminians] mean."[20]

The Remonstrants and Contra-Remonstrants lent their names to the religious and political factions in the growing tensions between the Arminians and the Gomarists. One side stressed tolerant discussion and the mutual acceptance of persons of differing viewpoints. The other demanded obligatory adherence to a rigid and narrow formulation of Theodore Beza's theology, a systematic version of Calvin's theology, now defined by Gomarus and his allies. A key feature of Arminian moderation was the position that dogmatic statements should be limited to essentials and that many topics in theology that were not explicitly treated in the Bible should be considered indeterminate and open to scholarly discussion and disagreement. This toleration of dissent was a denial of the axiom that proper reasoning could resolve all ambiguities, that Reformed doctrine could be exhaustively and permanently codified, leaving no room for disagreement. Taking the Bible as sole authority in matters of doctrine, the Arminians wanted to subject the Belgic Confession and the Heidelberg Catechism (two principal foundations of Reformed theology) to biblical critique and, where necessary, modify and improve them. Gomarists asserted that these documents, being derived solely from Scripture, displayed complete consistency with Scripture. As it happened, Robinson and the Pilgrims agreed with the Remonstrants in not accepting the Belgic Confession as definitive and dogmatically binding (even though they did not disagree with its formulations).

The factionalism of high politics was reflected throughout society. By mid-August 1610, Leiden's predominantly Arminian town council was considering how best to extinguish what they called "the disunity that had arisen in religion concerning the doctrine of predestination, because disputatious gatherings were happening not only on street corners and in shops but also in the churches; and they seemed to be heading towards evil results—so much that they were calling each other's ministers false and uproarious."[21]

The government simply forbade such meetings on pain of arbitrary punishment—an empty gesture. Repeatedly, futilely, the town council resolved that the right of the States of Holland to legislate in matters of religion was to be maintained and that the Contra-Remonstrants should be obedient to that principle. At this time, Contra-Remonstrants rejected the idea that the Arminian civil government should supervise the church, so a command from city hall to be tolerant or be punished received no respect. The irony of such a command ("We will not tolerate intolerance!") seems to have gone unnoticed by all involved. Robinson's sympathies on such matters were clearly on the side of the anti-Arminians. The Pilgrims, who had suffered under the theocratic aspects of English government, could argue idealistically for the separation of church and state, mirroring a position favored by the Dutch anti-Arminians for practical rather than principled reasons.

In Leiden, the court had the final right in nominating Reformed clergy. Since the 1580s they had attempted to pacify religious factionalism with balanced appointments of ministers with opposing views. The burgomasters were also curators of the university, and they attempted to impose the same balance in the theology faculty. To succeed Jacob Arminius as professor of theology, in 1610, the University of Leiden appointed the German professor Conrad Vorstius. Arminius, Uytenbogaert, and Vorstius taught a moderate and evolving Calvinism in opposition to an increasingly strident and narrowing development of Calvinism as represented at Leiden by Gomarus and the minister Festus Hommius, who also held a faculty position. Robinson quickly became friends with Hommius.

Anti-Arminians reacted immediately to the nomination of Vorstius.[22] To prevent him from teaching, they accused him of being a heretic, particularly calling him a Socinian (that is to say, an anti-Trinitarian). Throughout the disputes between the Remonstrants and the Contra-Remonstrants, as also in the attacks on Arminius and Vorstius, the opponents of the more tolerant position that had characterized Dutch theological discussion since the sixteenth century propagandistically described their doctrines and theirs only as "orthodox." They called the ideas of Arminius and his followers innovations, implying that innovations as such were reprehensible and that their own views embodied an ancient and unalterable truth. Innovation—necessarily involving change—was imperfect, if inalterability was an aspect of perfection. Even though their set of syllogisms had been constructed recently, they thought that their conclusions were implied by the divinely inspired ancient texts and that, therefore, the truth defined by their ideas eternally predated creation. This constricted and rigid Reformed theology that the anti-Arminians claimed was the sole truth was first proclaimed "orthodox," however, by a national synod, at the Synod of Dort (Dort) in 1618–1619. Only then and there, alternative views on the same main positions were first officially declared to be heretical. Thus, any description of the disputes before 1618 that without qualification applies the word *orthodox* to describe the anti-Arminian, anti-Vorstian position is consequently anachronistic and either thoughtlessly or tendentiously so.[23] Arminius and Gomarus both stood within the Reformed Church. Their theological differences could still find a mutual home within that church, until Gomarus and his followers succeeded in narrowing the definitions of what could be discussed and tolerated and consequently succeeded in splitting the church.

Anti-Trinitarianism, on the other hand, was considered unorthodox by most other Christians, including the Reformed and the Church of England, as well as Robinson and the Pilgrims. Also called Socinianism (after an early anti-Trinitarian theologian, Faustus Socinus), this strand of Christian thought rigorously applied the rule of relying solely on Scripture. Although several passages suggest the concept of the Trinity, nowhere in the Bible is there an explicit reference to the Trinity. That 1 John 5:7-8 (the *Comma Johanneum*) is not found in any of the earliest Bible manuscripts

Conrad Vorstius, Arminius's would-be successor at Leiden. Courtesy of The Leiden American Pilgrim Museum.

and must be later a interpolation had been discovered by Erasmus; theologians knew this.[24] But only the anti-Trinitarians addressed the problem of trying to redefine their concept of God and of Jesus's relation to the Father consciously aware that the Trinitarian formulation was simply one dogmatic resolution adopted by a council (and, therefore, in their view, consequently subject to error).[25] Most Christians thought that the concept of the Trinity (like the entirety of Calvinism) was logically implied by the ancient texts of the Bible, even if not found in them. Hence, it was considered a truth that predated creation. Alternative logic was declared unorthodox and innovative.

The general rejection of this Bible-based anti-Trinitarian unorthodoxy meant that no better way to discredit a Reformed theologian existed than to accuse him of Socinianism. Vorstius assured people he was a Trinitarian, not a Socinian. His opponents claimed he was slyly concealing his true convictions. Matthew Slade, an English ex-Separatist from Amsterdam, had married the daughter of Amsterdam's violently anti-Arminian preacher Peter Plancius. Plancius publicly denounced Vorstius and the Arminians as endangering the purity of the Reformed Church. Slade alerted the English ambassador Sir Ralph Winwood to the anti-Arminian sentiments in Amsterdam. Slade even sent two packets of anti-Vorstian material to the Archbishop of Canterbury, George Abbott. The archbishop was so alarmed he sent these missives on by special messenger to the king.

King James I responded immediately with a letter to the States General (the Netherlands' protonational parliament). If they did not desist in their intention of hiring Vorstius as professor at Leiden, and if they did not subject Vorstius's books to public punishment, James I would declare himself and his country enemies of the Netherlands. To appear to support heresy was to invite divine wrath. (And he meant the wrath of a divinity who could destroy thirty towns in a single storm.) All Vorstius's books that could be found were ordered to be burnt on bonfires in London, Oxford, and Cambridge. If Vorstius took up his professorial position, no students from the Kingdom of England would be permitted to study at Leiden.

Ambassador Winwood delivered this ultimatum to the States General on September 21, 1611. Uytenbogaert, in the meantime, had been sent by the States of Holland to negotiate permission for

Vorstius to leave his professorate in Steinfurt to take up the position in Leiden. Among the numerous professors and ministers who wrote to recommend Vorstius was Leiden's professor of ethics, Peter Bertius, a friend who had delivered the oration at Arminius's funeral. Bertius had himself been in friendly contact with Socinians in previous years.[26]

When Vorstius came to The Hague, officials examining him found no objectionable responses to their questions; but a faction of ministers inspired by Plancius continued to accuse him of heresy. They started a letter-writing campaign to discredit Vorstius, while Slade stirred up opposition in England during travels there. Plancius requested letters from professors at Heidelberg to discredit Vorstius, Bertius, and others who shared Arminian ideas. An anti-Arminian professor at Franeker, Sybrandus Lubbertus, quickly produced anti-Vorstian pamphlets and books that Slade took along to officials in England.

In October 1611, King James wrote to the Dutch parliament expressing his annoyance that Vorstius had been allowed to move to Leiden. If heresy were not extirpated, he reminded them, they would suffer the malediction of God, infamy among all the Reformed churches, and perpetual schism and distraction in their body politic. Ambassador Winwood was instructed to insist on the removal of "this blasphemous Monster," and also to insist that they suppress "this licentious Liberty of disputing or arguing such unprofitable Questions...at Leyden as in all the rest of their Dominions."[27]

Why did King James's opinions matter? The period 1609–1621 was the Twelve Years' Truce in the Dutch revolt against Hapsburg domination. This time of peace came after the first half of what became known as the Eighty Years' War. After the assassination of Prince William the Silent, who led the revolt, the Dutch asked for English military aid, even offering to accept Queen Elizabeth as their sovereign. Although she cautiously refused, she sent large amounts of military assistance in men and supplies. The English ambassador, in contrast to all other foreign diplomats, was granted a seat on the Dutch Council of State, the country's highest government authority. The detailed lists of a general muster of the Dutch army, held in 1610, show that about 47 percent of the soldiers in the Dutch army were British.[28] The Dutch needed ongoing British assistance to defend their borders during the truce, besides major military aid in the event of the resumption of war. Imagining himself God's appointed defender of true theology, King James used the military circumstances to blackmail the Dutch into complying with his demands. When their response was not quick enough, he let it be known that a marriage between his son, Prince Charles (who would succeed him as King Charles I), and the daughter of the King of Spain might be an appropriate way to bring about religious and political peace. The Dutch had good reason to fear that the king might abandon their cause.

Robinson and the Pilgrims had reason to fear English interference in the Netherlands, which could affect the religious freedom they enjoyed. Simultaneously, the danger of Spanish Hapsburg victory and suppression of all Protestantism loomed as a real threat to their future. The shifting political developments, as expressed in King James's intervention in the superficially benign issue of a professorial appointment in theology at Leiden, contributed to the urgency of the Pilgrims' quandary about whether they should stay in Holland or move elsewhere.

The charge that Vorstius was still a Socinian (as if it were obvious that he had been previously), came from a Jesuit, Martin Becanus. He denounced all Protestant theology, demonstrating with syllogisms that Protestant positions implied various heresies. Anyone believing the premises, he claimed, implicitly must hold the conclusions he had derived from them. Connecting Socinus with Vorstius, and linking Vorstius with theological opinions previously published by King James I, Becanus asserted that the logical consequence of the shared presuppositions and their implications, as he demonstrated them, was atheism. By implication, King James I was a Socinian atheist (whom Catholics should dethrone).

Vorstius responded by denying that his thought implied Socinian anti-Trinitarianism. While he had not spoken in support of Socinianism, he had considered Socinus's thought important to study. Arminius, too, had in class discussed the ideas of several non-Calvinist thinkers, including Faustus Socinus and Sebastian Castellio.[29] (Castellio had argued that the concept of "orthodoxy" historically was nothing more than a polemical weapon with which a dominant party could easily condemn opponents.) Vorstius, similarly, thought it his duty as a theologian to be familiar with the writings of every other theologian whose works he could obtain, if only to refute them. Against an increasingly narrow Calvinist scholasticism,

Vorstius claimed freedom of theological discussion, the *libertas prophetandi* that John Robinson defended even for thoughtful laymen under the term *prophecy*.

Others were stung by Becanus's syllogisms. King James wanted nothing to do with the dangerous professor Vorstius, whom his ambassador called "the most remarkable Atheist which our Age hath borne."[30] The king informed the States General that continued alliance with England was "in no way compatible with the atheisms and heresies of Conrad Vorstius." What especially enraged King James was Vorstius's book *De Deo*, or *De Attributis Dei*, of 1610.[31] Slade pointed out to the king that Vorstius had written that God, existing in time, is mutable and subject to the accidents of time.[32]

This represented an attempt to make sense of the theological axioms that Christ was both God and man, and that the God of the Bible is a living God who intervenes in history. Moreover, Vorstius, like his contemporaries, had been trying to account for what is found in the Bible as if each part had equal validity and was to be taken seriously as in some identifiable way true. Vorstius confronted biblical issues that have attracted attention in recent times, and he arrived at some positions similar to ideas animating the discussion of "open theism."

Predicating that God knows everything that can be known but that the future, not having yet happened, is not in the category of what can be known, even by God, this idea of mutability allowed for the possibility of free will and the consequent potential for a fall from grace. Arminius, however, did not go this far. As Carl Bangs notes, Arminius attempted to resolve the difficulty of foreknowledge: "Since foreknowledge is of future things, strictly speaking, there is no indefinite foreknowledge: for it is knowledge that is indefinite, not foreknowledge: for the particle 'fore' restricts the knowledge of possible things to the foreknowledge of *future* things, things that shall be."[33] Carl Bangs continues, "He [Arminius] has it quite backward. *Knowledge* is of *entities*; *foreknowledge* is of *possibilities*. The first is certain; the latter, contingent."

The idea of divine mutability allowed for divine emotions toward and divine responses to human choices, as described throughout the Bible. Vorstius had observed that in the Bible God is characterized with the affective terms "love, hate, fear, desire, joy, doubt, and such-like affects."[34] King James was especially incensed that Vorstius conceived of God as reacting with emotion to the human condition. He demanded that Vorstius be banished from Leiden and be judged by the churches by means of an international conference (in writing, by correspondence). This is the beginning of what became the Synod of Dort.

Eventually the curators of the university bowed to the extraordinary pressure, preventing Vorstius from taking up his job as professor and ensuring that he not live in Leiden, although they continued to pay his salary. In the meantime, Gomarus had resigned in protest of the appointment of Vorstius. Thus the university had two vacancies for the position of professor of theology. They appointed Johannes Polyander, who became a personal friend of John Robinson, and Simon Episcopius, who theologically was Arminius's successor. Robinson attended the lectures of both, evidently serving as an informer to the anti-Arminians of what Episcopius said (since anti-Arminian students boycotted the lectures).

Through a visit to England by the young Hugo Grotius, King James was convinced to argue for toleration. In March 1613, he informed the States General "that for the peace of those churches ...both sides should be enjoined not to meddle in their pulpits with those high points of predestination." Moreover, he felt that "both opinions might consist with the truth of Christianity and with the Salvation of men's souls."[35] The ministers should be expressly commanded, said the king, to maintain peace through mutual tolerance for diversity of opinion or feeling, at least until the public authority (the civil government) had determined otherwise. In January 1614, the States of Holland issued a decree imposing toleration and calling a halt to public dispute on the doctrine of predestination. This had little effect. Such toleration was so antithetical to the desires of the Contra-Remonstrants that they suspected the king had been tricked into signing a document with which he did not really agree.

1614–1619: THE ENGLISH CALL FOR DUTCH SEPARATISM AND A DUTCH SYNOD

When in 1610 John Robinson published his book *A Justification of Separation*, he had addressed a strikingly analogous situation to that facing the Dutch anti-Arminians. Though his ire was directed toward England's king, the States General also represented an instance of the civil authority of the reigning magistrate dominating the affairs of the church. In his newest book, *Of*

Religious Communion, Private, and Public (1614), Robinson turned his focus to the Dutch churches. Perhaps recalling the Revelator's warning to the church at Ephesus (2:4), Robinson laments that the Dutch churches have, "through continuance of time and peace...lost of their first purity and zeal."[36]

By the same token, Robinson took it upon himself to call the Dutch Reformed Church back to its old-time purity and zeal through a further separation. Robinson's justification for separating and the Pilgrims' example could provide inspiration for their Dutch friends who arrived at a similar conviction of the need to withdraw from the public church. Whether or not Dutch Separatism might have arisen in some hypothetical absence of contact with Robinson, he was, in fact, a friend of two leading anti-Arminian theologians (Hommius and Polyander) who urged withdrawal from the state-controlled Reformed Church. Unsurprisingly, they used the same biblical texts to support their opinions.

A rather close parallel with the experience of English Separatists occurred in The Hague. There a Contra-Remonstrant minister, Hendrik Rosaeus, was suspended by the States of Holland for refusing to serve together with Uytenbogaert. He refused to recognize the authority of the parliament that had suspended him. Instead, he led a breakaway congregation that came together in a nearby village, walking out of the town to hear him preach. To Contra-Remonstrants his obstinate intransigence appeared to deserve the respect due to a heroic martyr.

By the end of 1615, Contra-Remonstrants had withdrawn from the public Reformed Church and set up Separated congregations in Rotterdam, Gouda, Haarlem, The Hague, and five other towns. Both English and Dutch Separatists were seeking to recover what they considered the lost ideal purity of New Testament Christianity by withdrawing from what had become polluted by false doctrine. Robinson's Leiden friend Hommius demanded use of one of the two large churches in town for Contra-Remonstrants exclusively.

These factionalists objected to the appointment of a new Remonstrant minister who had written a pamphlet against killing heretics. That policy, as it happened, had been recently advocated in print by a Contra-Remonstrant minister in Rotterdam. The obvious target was Vorstius. Leiden's Contra-Remonstrants claimed that the new minister's stated opposition to judicial murder of heretics indicated his enmity toward Reformed churches. Calvinists killed far fewer than did Catholics, but, as the Contra-Remonstrants forthrightly asserted of themselves (and Calvin demonstrated), executing heretics was a real possibility.

Hommius judged the willingness to permit officially sanctioned murder to be a test of proper theological opinion regarding the authority of the civil magistrate. Remonstrants' denial of the magistrates' right to kill heretics was, wrote Hommius, in clear opposition to Article 36 of the Belgic Confession. Article 36 includes the opinion that the civil government should "remove every obstacle to the preaching of the gospel, and to every aspect of divine worship." The government was obliged to remove and destroy "all idolatry and false worship of the Antichrist." Leiden's burgomasters summoned the ministers and deacons to remind them that all had signed an agreement promising to work together in harmony. The civil authorities admonished the Contra-Remonstrants that that solemn undertaking should have more weight in their decisions than "the complaints of five or six agitated idiots."[37]

In the meantime, Slade had continued to urge intolerance in his correspondence with Ambassador Sir Dudley Carleton. He successfully effected a reversal of King James's opinion that toleration of dissent was not only possible but also, for the sake of peace in the land, obligatory. The king wrote again to the States General to demand a national synod be held. But now he expressed the belief that there is just one "sole and unique truth." He regretted that Vorstius had not been executed.

Authorities in The Hague attempted to restore unity. Rosaeus's Separatist congregation would be officially allowed to meet in the village church of Rijswijk near The Hague. That merely acknowledged and permitted a situation that had proceeded illicitly for nearly a year—with six or seven hundred people absenting themselves from church in The Hague to avoid contact with the Remonstrants. It was January, however, and, for convenience in bad weather, the Contra-Remonstrants demanded the use of a church in The Hague instead. Prince Maurits offered them the Great Church (Grote Kerk, St. Jacobskerk), to be shared with the Remonstrants. The Reformed consistory and the town government were willing to go along with this decision on condition that Rosaeus acknowledge his schismatic error and apologize. Rosaeus would have none of that, nor were his supporters intending to share a church with anyone. In their final service at Rijswijk,

January 22, 1617, the Dutch Separatists chose their own deacons and elders, ostentatiously creating a total schism from the established Reformed church, that now consisted solely of Remonstrants and people who wanted to remain neutral. The official Reformed consistory and church officers (all Remonstrants) consequently felt justified in refusing the use of the Grote Kerk to Rosaeus and his congregation. The confrontation was deadlocked.

On that same Sunday, a sixty-foot long whale died on the beach outside The Hague at Scheveningen, about five miles from Leiden. Many people understood such monsters to be portents of further major events. The great rift in the Reformed Church in The Hague might be marked by the heavens in this way, some thought. Among the hundreds of gawkers searching for meaning was the Mennonite historian and theologian, Pieter Twisck, who came with some friends all the way from Hoorn in North Holland.[38] Twisck was gathering material for a history of the world conceived as a history of the downfall of tyranny (eventually published in two volumes in 1619 and 1620).[39] The whale, however, was not Twisck's immediate goal. He had come first to Leiden to discuss theology with John Robinson. Two days of meetings in the presence of the entire Pilgrim congregation took place with the help of an interpreter.

Twisck may have wondered if the Pilgrims might become English-speaking Mennonites, as had many of the English Anabaptists in Amsterdam after their leader John Smyth died. The Pilgrims, however, disagreed with Mennonites on baptism and Christology. The Pilgrims, for example, retained infant baptism, believing the children of church members to be included in the new covenant (as an analogy to the covenant with Abraham and his seed forever). The Mennonites rejected that traditional concept of baptism in favor of what is now called "believer's baptism," requiring a personal statement of faith by someone capable of adult experience and understanding. Despite their disagreements, the visit introduced Robinson to the author of the first history or compendium of sentiments in favor of religious toleration. Twisck's book from 1609 was called *Religion's Freedom, A brief Chronological Description of the Foundation of Religion against the Coercion of Conscience, Drawn from Many Various Books from the Time of Christ to the Year 1609, From which One Can See Clearly...That the Steel Sword of the Wordly Government Does Not Extend over Conscience to the Compulsion of Belief; that Heretics and Disbelievers Must Not Be Con-*

verted with the Violence of the Worldly Government but with God's Word; That Variety of Religions Does Not Bring Decay or Disruption in a Country or City; That the Kingdom of Christ is Not of This World; And that the Gospel Does Not Have to be Defended with the Sword.[40]

Twisck's book warns against the danger that the Netherlands might slip into intolerant discord during the Twelve Years' Truce that began in 1609. Mutual toleration among Protestants had been a pragmatic necessity during the hostilities against the Spanish Hapsburgs. Mennonites feared for their future safety during peace. Robinson and his followers became noticeably more open to cautious toleration of other religious interpretations, echoing Twisck's logic regarding the consequences of the fall of humanity described in Genesis: If all humanity had become imperfect, then all theology, being human, was imperfect; and all assessment of theologies reflected imperfection of understanding. Consequently, one's own theology was necessarily imperfect, as one's understanding in general was imperfect. This perception, also adopted by the Remonstrants, taught that proper humility included the recognition that the person who might be wrong in an argument was oneself. Both Arminius and Episcopius urged mutual toleration based on the perception that all human opinion is imperfect, an opinion expressed earlier by Sebastian Castellio. Episcopius believed that only a few essential doctrines could be found in the Bible; all others should be open to differences in interpretation and tolerated peacefully.[41]

Humility was not a characteristic of the Dutch Separatists in The Hague. They refused to share a church with the Remonstrants. Ambassador Sir Dudley Carleton helped the Contra-Remonstrants by allowing them to move their services into the Gasthuiskerk, which had become the English Church. Carleton, as ambassador, was the leading layman. The English Church's minister was the well-known Calvinist theologian William Ames. By making the Gasthuiskerk available to Rosaeus's Separated congregation, Carleton interfered with Dutch government attempts to reestablish religious unity by bringing the Dutch Reformed congregation back together. Like the rotting whale, England's involvement in Dutch politics and religious controversy was huge but hard to measure. Additionally, English diplomatic pressure about continued military assistance, about silencing Vorstius, and about King James's demand that the Dutch hold a national synod must have played a part in convincing Count Maurits to choose publicly to support the Separated Dutch congregation of Rosaeus. Carleton wrote to Winwood (by this time Secretary of State) that "with his excellency [Maurits] I have had speech during this debate, and gave him the best comfort I could in supporting a good cause, which was found needful against so strong opposition."[42]

A few days later, sixteen Contra-Remonstrant ministers signed a formal resolution of separation. They organized committees of correspondence to coordinate their cause, to organize independent consistories, to agitate for recognition of their splinter groups as being the true church in contrast to the established Reformed Church from which they had separated, and to identify those people they would henceforth shun (Remonstrants and people who either supported the Remonstrants or attempted to remain neutral). Anti-Remonstrant riots, arson, and further unrest occurred in Amsterdam, Delft, Rotterdam, and elsewhere. Militia members were required to take new oaths of loyalty. Carleton informed Maurits and Johan van Oldenbarnevelt that King James wanted the Arminians suppressed. Van Oldenbarnevelt informed Carleton that the Contra-Remonstrants were the Dutch equivalents to England's Puritans, railing against the established Reformed Church. Carleton refused to acknowledge the traditionally tolerant position of Holland's Reformed Church, insisting that such toleration of theological discussion represented dangerous innovation.

Maurits had only recently become interested in the religious disputes. He called for a national synod just as King James had advised. Doing so, he was overturning the constitution of the United Provinces, which reserved to the individual provinces the right to determine religious issues, guaranteeing that no province would be dictated in that topic by any other province or combination of them. The unified nation (The United Provinces of the Netherlands) was practically called into existence (in a modern sense) by the assumptions underlying the convocation of the National Synod of Dort in 1618–1619. But the way to the national synod was a path of increasing conflict with the historic rights and privileges of individual provinces, particularly of Holland and Utrecht; and the way to the synod was a progress of increasingly clear support for the Contra-Remonstrants by Maurits, under unremitting pressure from King James, and of steadily fiercer opposition to the traditionalist policies of van Oldenbarnevelt. King James forbade his subjects to send their children to study at the University of Leiden, to prevent their falling into Arminian or Vorstian errors. In the spring of 1617, Maurits demonstratively attended services with the Contra-Remonstrants, and he dismissed his court chaplain, the Remonstrant Johan Uytenbogaert.

In the summer of 1617, the magistrates of Leiden, Utrecht, and other Remonstrant towns hired extra guards to protect themselves from the increasing insolence of Contra-Remonstrant mobs. Leiden's new guards moved into position in front of the town hall on October 2, to forestall disturbances expected during the militia exercises that were part of the annual celebrations on October 3, commemorating the lifting of the Siege of Leiden in 1574. Jeering youths provoked a quarrel with the guards, who shot in the air, accidentally killing a wealthy burgher who was watching from an upstairs window. Carleton reported that "another was killed the night following in the streets; one of the soldiers beaten to death likewise with stones, and divers hurt."[43] The militia, summoned to suppress the riot, refused to disperse, demanding the dismissal of the new guards. Instead, the magistrates ordered barricades to be built across the main street at each end of the city hall. With cannons aimed both ways in the street, the new guards were expected to protect the government from insurrection. The barricade became known as the Arminian Redoubt.

Three days after the rioting in Leiden, Ambassador Carleton delivered a message to the States General, expressing the king's views against Arminius and the Remonstrants, denouncing the establishment of the new companies of guards as inevitably destructive of national unity, and demanding once again that the disagreements in religion and divisions in politics be subjected to the judgment of a national synod. By November no action had yet been taken; the king retaliated by letting it be known that he had given up on the Netherlands. He could not rely on such a disunited country that was likely to fall into the hands of Spain, so he had decided to proceed further with the negotiations for having his son marry the daughter of the King of Spain. The Dutch saw that they could not rely on the king to help defend them against Spain.

The Remonstrant leaders and Vorstius withdrew from public appearance for a few weeks. They were collaborating on a seventy-one page response brought out in mid-November called *The Balance, for Properly Considering in all Appropriateness the Oration, of the*

Noble, Highly Learned, Wise, Perspicacious Gentleman, Milord Dudley Carleton, Ambassador of the Illustrious King of Great Britain, recently Given in the Meeting of the Noble Highly Powerful Lords States General: Made for a Thorough Indication of the Origin, &c., of the present Disunities in the Church and in Politics: and for a Defense of those who are Innocent therein.[44] Slade and Carleton, and through them, King James, thought Grotius was the principal author. Grotius and van Oldenbarnevelt were so closely associated with the text that they could not escape the anger of Carleton, when he discovered himself personally ridiculed in the book. Carleton transferred the insult to proclaim it an affront to the royal majesty of King James.

The Balance complained that the ambassador had involved himself in three subjects about which he was ill informed—the doctrines of Arminius, Dutch law, and the limits of Reformed theology. The author had no wish to offend either the ambassador or the king, he wrote, and he claims to overlook (while mentioning) the erroneous title to Carleton's oration, which asserted that the present disunity in church and state had arisen as a consequence of Arminius's doctrine. With polite circumlocutions, the author indicates that the ambassador was too ignorant to have opened his mouth, much less to interfere in Dutch politics. *The Balance* provides evidence that what had become known as the Arminian or Remonstrant doctrine had a long history among earlier Dutch Reformed theologians, as well as theologians elsewhere. Carleton claimed that the Arminians' request for toleration and protection, in their Remonstrance of 1610, was an attempt to introduce their theology by force. On the contrary, *The Balance* pointed out that Remonstrants considered it "impermissible for a Christian to introduce his opinion through force." Moreover, the Remonstrants "heartily wished that the Contra-Remonstrants would agree with them on this—instead of practicing the killing of heretics, an action that demonstrated that they were the ones who really wanted to introduce their doctrines everywhere by force."[45] Carleton called the Arminians anarchists, but, as *The Balance* indicated, it was the Contra-Remonstrants who intended to depose the magistrates who favored toleration. Who, then, were the anarchists? No Remonstrants were calling for murder of their opponents, but Contra-Remonstrant pamphlets promised to kill Arminians for small change.

The Balance closes with a quotation from a letter King James had sent to the States General not long before, in which the king commented that "experience had taught him that such differences are ended very badly in the disputes of theologians, but that they were much more appropriately decided by public authority" (by the civil magistrates, in other words, who were predominantly Arminian).[46]

English response was swift. Matthew Slade described *The Balance* as "lewdly and traitorously written."[47] Carleton was furious, not only at being made a fool of himself, but also for the disrespect shown to the king's majesty. How dare the Remonstrants point out that the ambassador's most recent royal messages contradicted what the king had written previously to the States General and expressed the complete opposite of royal policy when dealing with Puritans in England and Presbyterians in Scotland! Carleton appeared before the States General and demanded that the publication be suppressed and all copies destroyed and that those who had written and distributed the libel be punished. Censorship was thus introduced in the Netherlands under this diplomatic pressure, first against the Remonstrants, and then against the Pilgrims, whose books also attacked the religious policies of King James.

Carleton also demanded the destruction of all copies of a political broadsheet, also called *The Balance*. Symbolically, a great weigh-scale is shown with the theological works of Arminius on one side and Calvin's *Institutes* on the other. Arminius stands beside his books, which have the additional weight on them of the fur-lined robes of the magistrates. Gomarus stands by the other side of the scales, where Calvin's *Institutes* are shown. Presiding over the scene, in the background, we see King James of England. It is Calvin's *Institutes* that have the greater weight, but

Op de WAAG-SCHAAL.

The Balance. Courtesy of The Leiden American Pilgrim Museum.

that is only because Prince Maurits stands beside Calvin's book and lays the weight of his sword next to it on the scale-pan.

Soon after the publication of the two versions of *The Balance*, Prince Maurits led a military coup, removing Remonstrants from the government. The Synod of Dort was convened, with the Remonstrants treated as accused. Here we shall not treat further of the Synod. Only in the eyes of the triumphant Contra-Remonstrants did it bring about the triumph of some true "orthodox" doctrine; in the opinion of others, then and now, it merely reached the decisions required of it by King James, which assured the Dutch of continued military support in the ongoing revolt.

CONCLUSION

The stated purpose of the volume in which this chapter appears is to move us beyond simple caricatures of Arminius and of the persons who stood with him and against him during and after his death. Here we have traced the rise of an anti-Arminian religious and political faction that came to dominate Dutch society in the decade following the death of Arminius. In following the events, we have made the acquaintance of John Robinson and Conrad Vorstius, neither of whom has been given much attention previously in this context.

Robinson, a former student of William Perkins and the minister of the Pilgrims in Leiden, attended the lectures in the University of Leiden given by both the Arminians and the anti-Arminians. Explicitly anti-Arminian in his opinions about predestination, he nonetheless adopted a careful attitude toward human imperfection that led him and the Pilgrims to join with the Remonstrants in refusing to make adherence to the Heidelberg Catechism and the Belgic Confession obligatory. As we remarked at the beginning of this essay, Robinson was confident that "the Lord had more truth and light yet to break forth out of his holy Word."[48] The Leiden conflicts may be considered the underlying inspiration for Robinson's advice to his followers that they should not allow their religion to ossify in the form of his teaching or of the doctrines of earlier theologians.

Similarly pursuing more insight into the illuminating truth of the Bible, Vorstius developed a biblical conception of God that incorporated responsive emotion and, consequently, development. He was looking at the Bible without the philosophical presupposition that immutability must be a characteristic of perfection. On the one hand, Vorstius's description of the divine was consistent with the Arminian position on the question of free will and perseverance. On the other hand, Vorstius's ideas attracted the ire of King James I, whose intervention in the Dutch disputes proved immensely influential, guiding along politically determined lines the outcome of the Synod of Dort.

Robinson's caution regarding dogmatic formulations bore fruit in Plymouth Colony, when magistrates proposed complete religious toleration in 1645.[49] Vorstius's insight that God is described in the Bible as subject to interactive change adumbrates questions that have re-arisen in process theology and open theism. Predestination was inescapably a central issue for both Robinson and Vorstius, as it had been for Arminius and Gomarus. As Carl Bangs wrote about Arminius's formulation of predestination, "It was at this point that Arminius' colleague in Leiden, Gomarus, would raise serious questions. The present-day theologian will raise still more."[50]

NOTES

1. Edward Winslow, *Hypocrisie Unmasked* (London: John Bellamy, 1646), 97.
2. Ibid.
3. For a far more detailed exploration of this subject, see Jeremy Dupertuis Bangs, *Strangers and Pilgrims, Travellers and Sojourners—Leiden and the Foundations of Plymouth Plantation* (Plymouth, Mass.: General Society of Mayflower Descendants, 2009). For Robinson's relation to English Calvinist thought, see Timothy George, *John Robinson and the English Separatist Tradition* (Macon, Ga.: Mercer University Press, 1982); and Stephen Brachlow, *The Communion of Saints: Radical Puritan and Separatist Ecclesiology, 1570–1625* (Oxford: Oxford University Press, 1988).
4. Registrum Vagum Anthony Harrison, I, Norfolk Record Society, xxxii, 34–36, 156–59, cited and quoted in George, *John Robinson and the English Separatist Tradition*, 69–71.
5. *Exam. Perk.*, in *Works*, 3:249–484.
6. The quotation is found in William Barlow's *The Summe and Substance of the Conference...at Hampton Court*, published in Edward Cardwell, ed., *History of the Conferences*, 186, quoted in H. C. Porter, *Reformation and Reaction in Tudor Cambridge*, 2d ed. (Hamden, Conn.: The Shoe String Press, Archon Book, 1972), 406.
7. John Robinson, *A Manumission to a Manuduction*...(s.l.: s.n., 1615), 20–21.

8. Ibid.

9. University of Nottingham, Presentments Project, AN/PB 292/1–9; AN/PB 292/46 (Scrooby, 1598).

10. William Bradford, *Bradford's History "Of Plimoth Plantation,"* From the Original Manuscript (Boston: Wright & Potter, 1901), 11–15.

11. William Jones, *God's Warning to His People of England. By the Great Overflowing of the Waters...* (London: W. Barley and Io. Bayly, 1607).

12. John Robinson, *A Ivstification of Separation from the Church of England...* (s.l. [Amsterdam]: s.n. [Giles Thorp], 1610).

13. On Zabarella, see William F. Edwards, "The Logic of Iacopo Zabarella (1533–1589)" (Ph.D. diss., Columbia University, 1960); John Norman Randall, Jr., "The Development of Scientific Method in the School of Padua," *Journal of the History of Ideas* 1 (1940): 177–206; further, the articles by Heikki Mikkeli in the *Stanford Encyclopedia of Philosophy*, published online.

14. Champlin Burrage, ed., *An Answer to John Robinson of Leyden by a Puritan Friend, Now First Published from a Manuscript of A.D. 1609*, Harvard Theological Studies 9 (Cambridge, Mass.: Harvard University Press, 1920), 4.

15. John Robinson, *The Works of John Robinson, Pastor of the Pilgrim Fathers...*, ed. Robert Ashton (London: John Snow, 1851), 1:47.

16. William Whitaker (William Fitzgerald, trans.), *A Disputation on Holy Scripture, Against the Papists...* (Cambridge University Press, 1849), 449; see also 275–378, 447–66.

17. Bradford, *Bradford's History "Of Plimoth Plantation,"* 239.

18. *Exam. Perk.*, in *Works*, 3:281; see also p. 352, where Arminius describes Perkins's views thus: "Sin is connected necessarily with God's decree, nay, is dependent on it, so that man cannot but sin; otherwise there would be no room for that decree. Hence it follows, that since God has ordained men to sin, but has absolutely decreed to punish sin in many, He has simply destined most men to the fire of hell."

19. Bradford, *Bradford's History "Of Plimoth Plantation,"* 28.

20. John Robinson, *A Defence of the Doctrine Propounded by the Synod at Dort* (s.l.: s.n., 1624), 60–61.

21. Cornelis van Weesp, *Memoriael ofte gheheuchnis boeck* (ms. in the library of the Regionaal Archief Leiden), 3–4.

22. Gerard Brandt, *Historie der Reformatie, en andre Kerekelyke Geschiedenissen, in en omtrent de Nederlanden* (Amsterdam: Jan Rieuwertsz., Henrik and Dirk Boom, 1674), 2:146–47.

23. This is discussed more extensively in Jeremy Bangs, *Strangers and Pilgrims*, 472–75.

24. Calvin acknowledges that the word *Trinity* does not appear in the Bible. He further admits that "heretics may snarl and the excessively fas-

tidious carp at the word Person as inadmissible, in consequence of its human origin." Ridiculing his opponents, Calvin asks, "In regard to those parts of Scripture which, to our capacities, are dark and intricate, what forbids us to explain them in clearer terms?" (Calvin, *Institutes of the Christian Religion*, trans Henry Beveridge [Grand Rapids: Eerdmans, 1994], I.13.3).

25. Besides the brief discussion in Jeremy Bangs, *Strangers and Pilgrims*, 218–20, 475–86, see George Huntston Williams, *The Radical Reformation* (London: Weidenfeld and Nicolson, 1962); Martin Mulsow and Jan Rohls, eds., *Socinianism and Arminianism, Antitrinitarians, Calvinists, and Cultural Exchange in Seventeenth-Century Europe* (Leiden: Brill, 2005).

26. See Carl Bangs and Jeremy Bangs, "The Remonstrants and the Socinian Exiles in Holland," in *The Proceedings of the Unitarian Universalist Historical Society, Unitarianism in its Sixteenth and Seventeenth Century Settings, Papers Delivered at Meetings of the Society for Reformation Research* 20:II (1985–1986), 105–13.

27. The Hague, Nationaal Archief, Staten Generaal, 1550–1796 (toegangs nr. 1.01.04), inv. nr. 5885, Folder for 1611: Letter from James I [foliated in pencil, 67–70], [inscribed:] Date 6 October, Recep. 5 November 1611; Edmund Sawyer, ed., *Memorials of Affairs of State in the Reign of Q. Elizabeth and K. James I...*, 3 vols. (London: W. B. for T. Ward, 1725), 3:295, From the King to Sir Ralph Winwood, Oct. 6, 1611.

28. Simon Stevin, *Castrametatio, Dat is Legermeting* (Rotterdam: Ian van Waesberche, 1617).

29. Caspar Sibelius, a former student of Arminius, listed authors he remembered having been treated in Arminius's lectures in 1608: Calvin, Beza, Zanchius, Peter Martyr, Ursinus, Piscator, Perkins, and others including Socinus, Acontius, Castellio, Aquinas, Molina, and Suarez. See Gemeentearchief Deventer. 101 H 16, 17, 18 KL. (3 vols.): Caspar Sibelius, Ms. "De curriculo totiu vitae et peregrinationis suae historica narratio," I, 51.

30. Sawyer, *Memorials of Affairs of State*, 3:309–11: Sir Ralph Winwood's Protestation in the Assembly of the States General concerning Vorstius, Dec. 9, 1611 (Old Style); Sir Ralph Winwood to Mr. Trumbull (English Resident in Brussels), from The Hague, Dec. 12, 1611 (Old Style).

31. Conrad Vorstius, *Tractatus theologicus de Deo, sive de natura & attributis Dei...* (Steinfurt: Theoph. Cæsar, 1606; amplified edition 1610).

32. See Frederick Shriver, "Orthodoxy and Diplomacy: James I and the Vorstius Affair," *The English Historical Review* 85 (1970): 456. The king's objections were published in Dutch translation: *Oratie Ghedaen door den doorluchtighen/ eerentvesten/ welgeborenen Heere Rudolphus VVinwood Ridder/...Aengaende de beroepinghe Conradi Vorstij, tot de professie der H. Theologie in de Universiteyt tot Leyden* (s.l.: s.n., 1611), fol. Aii verso; quoting from Vorstius, *De Attributis Dei*, 212, 208–9, "Deus est alterabilis, mutabilis,

accidentibus subjectus. Godt is alteratie ende veranderinghe ende toevallen onderworpen." For developments of this concept of God, see Lucien Laberthonnière, *Le Réalisme Chrétien et l'Idéalisme Grec* (Paris: P. Lethielleux, 1904), and the works of Nicholas Berdyaev, Alfred North Whitehead, Charles Hartshorne, Bernard Loomer, Bernard Meland, and subsequent process theologians.

33. C. Bangs, 353, quoting *Exam. Gom., Works*, 3:535.

34. Vorstius, *De Attributis Dei*, 420–21: "Proprie attribuuntur Deo in sacris literis, Amor, odium, metus, desiderium, gaudium, desperatio, & similes affectiones. Godt wort eyghentlijck inde heylighe Schriftuere toegheschreven Liefde/ haet/ vreese/ begheerte/ blijschap/ vertwyffelinghe ende dierghelijcke affecten."

35. Sawyer, *Memorials of Affairs of State*, 3:451–52.

36. John Robinson, *Of Religious Commvnion Private & Publique*...(s.l. [Amsterdam]: s.n., 1614).

37. Van Weesp, *Memoriael ofte gheheuchnis boeck*, 50–57; 55: "alsoo de voorgaende acte meer behoorde te pondereeren als t'gecrijt van vyf, ses onrustighe idioten." Van Weesp, a Remonstrant magistrate, was referring to complaints from Contra-Remonstrants, whom he considered idiots.

38. Keith L. Sprunger, "The Meeting of Dutch Anabaptists and English Brownists, Reported by P. J. Twisck," in *The Contentious Triangle, Church, State and University, A Festschrift in Honor of Professor George Huntston Williams*, ed. Rodney Petersen and Calvin Augustine Pater, *Sixteenth Century Essays & Studies* 51 (Kirksville, Mo.: Thomas Jefferson University Press, 1999), 221–31.

39. Pieter Jansz. Twisck, *Chronijck vanden Onderganc der Tirannen* (Hoorn: Sacharias Cornelissen, I (1617/1619); II (1620)). The date "1617" is visibly altered on the engraved title page of the first volume.

40. Pieter Twisck, *Religions Vryheyt* (Hoorn: s.n., 1609).

41. Simon Episcopius, *Uytlegginge Over het vijfde Capittel des H. Euangelisten Mattheus, Vervatet in XXXIV. Predicatien Gedaen in de Christelijke Vergaderinge der Remonstranten*, ed. Philippus van Limborch (Franeker: Jacob Pieters, 1666), 153–55, 430–31; Episcopius, *Opera Theologica*, 2d ed. (London: Ex Officinia Mosis Pitt, 1678), second pagination sequence, 183–86, in "Examen Thesium Theologicarum Jacobi Capelli [. . .] De Controversiis quæ Fœderatum Belgium Vexant"—sections "De Tolerantia fraterna, Et de prophetandi libertate. Quam Tolerantiam perierint Remonstrantes." This is the edition also owned by John Locke: see John Harrison and Peter Laslett, *The Library of John Locke*, 2d ed. (Oxford: The Clarendon Press, 1971), 130n1060. The first edition of Episcopius, *Opera Theologica*, appeared in Amsterdam: Ioannis Blaev, 1650. See further, Jeremy Bangs, "Dutch Contributions to Religious Toleration," *Church History* 79 (2010): 585–613.

42. Lord Royston, Earl of Harwich, ed., *The Letters from and to Sir Dud-*

ley Carleton... January 1615/16 to December 1620, 3d ed. (London: s.n., 1780), 86–90.

43. Royston, *The Letters from and to Sir Dudley Carleton*, 183–86, Sept. 29 (Old Style), 1617, Carleton to Winwood.

44. *Weegh=Schael Om in alle billickheydt recht te over-vveghen de Oratie van... Dvdley Carleton* (s.l.: s.n., 1617).

45. *Weegh=Schael*, 14–15.

46. *Weegh=Schael*, 71; the king's letter is quoted from *Copie van den Brief des Conings van Groot Brittanien Ghescreven aen de E. M. Heeren Staten Generael des Gheunieerde Provincien VVaer in hy zijn Advijs, nopende het different tusschen de Remonstranten ende Contra-Remonstranten over-schrijft* (s.l.: s.n., 1613).

47. Willem Nijenhuis, *Matthew Slade, 1569–1628, Letters to the English Ambassador* (Leiden: Brill/Leiden University Press, for the Sir Thomas Browne Institute, 1986), 66.

48. Winslow, *Hypocrisie Unmasked*, 97.

49. This is discussed in Jeremy Bangs, "Dutch Contributions to Religious Toleration."

50. C. Bangs, 219.

CHAPTER 4

THE LOSS OF ARMINIUS IN WESLEYAN-ARMINIAN THEOLOGY

W. Stephen Gunter

Whether in common parlance, academic circles, or denominational literature, Methodist and Holiness folks in recent decades have increasingly taken up the habit of speaking of "Wesleyan theology" in place of the previously more common designation of "Wesleyan-Arminian theology." The contemporary resurgence of scholarly attention to Arminius may help to turn this popular tide. Still, it must be said that the removal of Arminius—particularly his soteriology—from Wesleyan theology was a long, long time in the making. The decade immediately following the death of Arminius already saw his soteriology disappearing from view. Both his posthumous supporters, the Remonstrants, and their opponents, the Contra-Remonstrants, played significant roles in this displacement. The trend continued as so-called Arminianism traveled to England, found common cause with Cambridge Platonism, and was adapted to suit Latitudinarian ecclesiastical views and policies. John Wesley's literary acquaintance with Arminius was minimal, but Wesley was largely faithful to the Dutchman's soteriology. But the 1770 Methodist Minutes controversy and John

Fletcher's consequently polemical and broadly influential *Checks against Antinomianism* led to the enduring, effective loss of Arminius's soteriology among the "Wesleyan-Arminians."

ARMINIUS THE REMONSTRANT: THE BURIAL OF ARMINIUS LEADING UP TO DORT

The year after Arminius's death in 1609, his widow and children published his *Declaration of Sentiments*. The publication of this *Verclaringhe* in 1610 was an attempt to honor him, but it was also a literary step toward vindicating him.[1] But even Arminius's family could not have anticipated that the decade of 1610–1620 would turn into a barrage of publications that was nothing less than rhetorical, theological warfare. Think of the situation as something akin to a presidential election debate that lasted almost ten years, with the decision on election finally coming at the Synod at Dort in 1618–1619—in this case an *eternal* election. Precise and carefully worded truth assertions would get lost in the rhetoric needed to score points and win followers.[2]

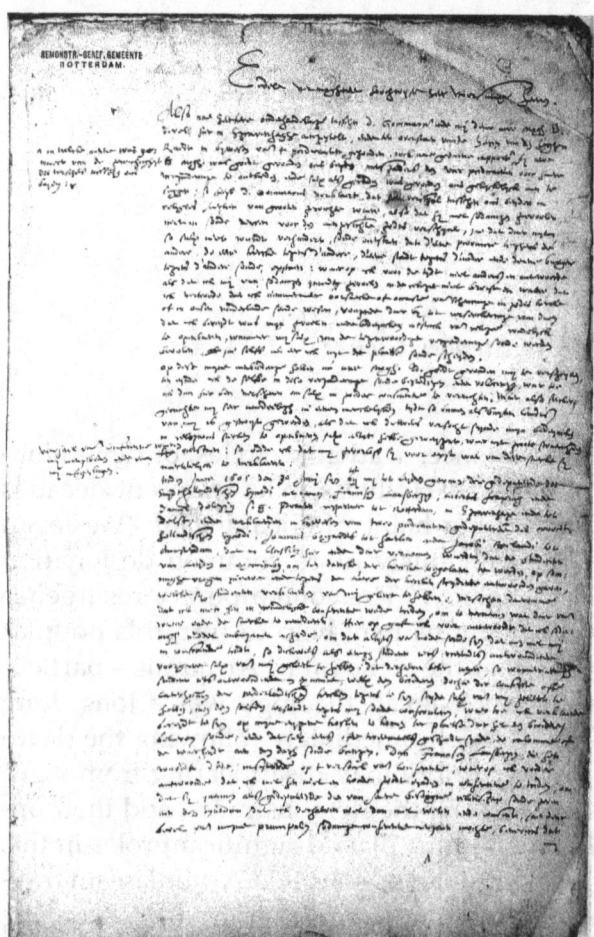

A page from the original manuscript of Arminius's *Declaration of Sentiments*. Courtesy of The Leiden American Pilgrim Museum.

This decade of pamphleteering resulted in a first phase of losing Arminius from sight so that, by the time the Synod of Dort convened in November 1618, it was in fact a form of altered Arminianism that was on trial. Indeed, it was an Arminianism altered in ways that Arminius likely would not have approved. If we have lost a true Arminianism—that is, an actual reflection of his theological sentiments—then that process of loss began very early after his death. If one may speak of guilt in this process of loss, then blame may be laid at the feet of both the Arminians (i.e., the Remonstrants) and the so-called Calvinists (i.e., the Contra-Remonstrants).[3] Put simplistically, the Remonstrants protested against a strict doctrine of double predestination and the Contra-Remonstrants (Arminius's nemesis, Francis Gomarus, chief among them) upheld and defended the dogma. Behind the scenes there was an additional doctrinal subtext at play regarding assumptions about sin and the interplay between faith and works. These theological disputes were carried on amid a highly complex set of social, political, and religious factors at work in the Netherlands:

1. The role of civil officials in ordering the life of the church;
2. The nature of the church as an inclusive or exclusive body;
3. The relationship of the confessional standards to church life;
4. The authority of Scripture and the creeds; and
5. The relationship between human freedom and divine sovereignty.[4]

To be sure, the issues are complex. The bond holding together the Republic of the Lowlands after a successful liberation of the country from Spain was a fragile one. Michael Adam Hakkenberg has noted "the Dutch Republic...did not yet have a strong central government, and it was constantly threatened by particularism and political fragmentation."[5] The comprehensive volatility in the Dutch context was not merely a difference over dogma inside the church; it was a complex set of differences that threatened the unity of the nation. Put another way, it was more than the reputation of Arminius that was on the line. He was a casualty on the way to redefining the boundaries of political and religious authority. If one looks only at the formal doctrinally contested points of the warring parties, one misses the volatile republican nature of the rhetorical warfare. It was this pamphlet warfare—somewhat analogous to political action committee advertisements—that drove the agenda in the first decade after Arminius's death when the distinctive emphases of his soteriology began to be lost from view.

Ever since the Synod at Dort, even well-versed historians and theologians have tended to view the theological scene in the Netherlands through the lens of that great synod and see the country as essentially Calvinist. While this was slowly but increasingly true after 1620, it certainly was not the case in prior decades. The Lowlands were religiously and theologically eclectic. Arminius's teachings were not far out of step with the perspective of many leading voices, especially at the national leadership level. Even by the time of the Synod of Dort, barely one third of the general Dutch population was Protestant, and not all these were strict Calvinists. The general population moved very slowly away from traditional Roman Catholic beliefs.[6] The Anabaptists (especially Mennonites) were present and active, although they never organized in ways that made them politically powerful. Nevertheless, their doctrinal inclinations permeated the theological climate. They were not doctrinaire in any exclusive way, and they certainly were not strictly predestinarians.

It is not an exaggeration to say that toleration (officially affirmed at the Union of Utrecht in 1579) and eclecticism were prevailing inclinations. When forty-five ministers gathered in 1610 at The Hague under the supervision of the court preacher, Johannes Uytenbogaert, to formulate their theological opinions in a formal petition for recognition known as the Remonstrance, they were not necessarily doing anything subversive or revolutionary. Theirs was a formal petition to the States of Holland for official recognition and, where necessary, protection against the intolerance and attacks of the strict Calvinists. Interesting to note is that these Arminians, although perhaps a minority in the Dutch Reformed Church as a whole, were actually in a majority among the magistrates in many larger cities. So the magistrates in those cities took care to appoint Arminian ministers.

In the five points of the Remonstrance of 1610, Arminius's influence is clear: Phrasing of key points was taken directly from the theological affirmations in his *Declaration of Sentiments*.[7] This formal request for protection stirred the political and ecclesial waters to such an extent that in December of 1610 the States of Holland called for a conference in The Hague. Rather than cooling the temperatures of the opposing parties, the conflict between the Remonstrants and the Contra-Remonstrants only intensified. The five articles of the Remonstrance were answered with the five articles of the Contra-Remonstrance. The controversy was now beginning to heat up in the public arena with an open division of parties. From this point on we begin to lose sight of Arminius himself, as well as certain important aspects of his theology.

Rather quickly thereafter, towns across the Republic came to identify with one party or the other, while some were divided internally—part Remonstrant and part Contra-Remonstrant. With astonishing speed, the driving issues became territorial, centering on positions of power and influence in pulpits and in positions of civil governance. In 1614 the States of Holland, *without* the support of Amsterdam and other Contra-Remonstrant inclined cities, adopted the "Resolution for Peace in the Churches." This resolution condemned the extreme positions on either side of the issue:

1. That God "created any man unto damnation," or
2. That man "of his own natural powers or deeds can achieve salvation."[8]

This further stipulated, in an attempt to protect the Remonstrants, that those who refused to affirm the five articles of the Contra-Remonstrance were not to be subject to slander and attacks, but were, instead, to be tolerated in the churches.

The Resolution for Peace was anything but, as it failed to satisfy either side in the squabble. At this point the story gets complicated by scenarios of unintended consequences. The Amsterdam classis (a local council of ministers), dominated now by anti-Arminian sentiment, blatantly refused to follow the directives of the resolution and began openly to support Contra-Remonstrant groups who wished to hold separate worship services in towns where Remonstrant ministers were appointed. Thus, the resolution was increasingly interpreted as an instrument in support of the Arminians. When powerful church leaders openly defied the intent of the resolution, the government was faced with a difficult decision: to enforce or not to enforce. The advocate general, Oldenbarnevelt, chose to enforce the state's authority "to use their supreme power to dismiss, or make the towns dismiss, any ministers infringing the resolution."⁹ In principle, this meant that action could be taken against both Remonstrants and Contra-Remonstrants, but it was in practice the Contras who suffered the most. In a majority (or at least a significant plurality) of towns, the civil magistrates were Arminians. Thus it was the Contra-Remonstrant ministers, often against the wishes of the local congregation itself, who were dismissed for violating the Resolution for Peace.

The controversy was so heated that, in 1616, in The Hague, Rev. Henricus Rosaeus refused to celebrate communion with his Remonstrant colleague, Uytenbogaert, who was chaplain to the Senate. When Rosaeus was dismissed from his ministerial office, he went to the neighboring village of Rijswijk, and every Sunday a large group of his supporters walked several kilometers from The Hague to Rijswijk to hear him preach. In numerous other towns and villages, Contra-Remonstrant ministers were dismissed and replaced with Remonstrant ministers, almost always against the wishes of their congregations. Even in towns where sentiment was pro-Arminian, civil magistrates forcing out the parish minister was not welcomed.¹⁰ The Contra-Remonstrants began to separate from the public churches and to establish their own churches, calling their own ministers without the "interference" of civil magistrates.

By 1617 the situation in the Lowlands had devolved into what the poet Jacob Cats describes as "the year of violence."¹¹ The policy of "mutual toleration" had resulted in almost comprehensive "mutual condemnation and reprisal." Both sides struggled to turn popular opinion in their favor, but the struggle was increasingly characterized by violence: "In the pulpits and the taverns, on the streets...in high places and low, were heard the violent discussions in which no bitter term was spared. The quarrel threatened the existence of the young nation. The academic discussion of Gomarus and Arminius had become [the] bone of contention that divided Holland into two hostile camps."¹²

One cluster of events stands out in its symbolic importance. As mentioned previously, the Contra-Remonstrants in The Hague were walking to an adjacent village to hear their preacher, Henricus Rosaeus, who had been forced out of his pulpit in The Hague. Prince Maurits had heretofore remained aloof from the fray by supporting the official government decision of "mutual" toleration. But his neutrality changed in 1617. In January, the Contra-

Remonstrants of The Hague returned to the city for worship in the home of a layman. The States of Holland formally requested Prince Maurits, as commander of the army, to enforce government policy to keep the church from meeting. But the Prince refused, saying that his actual responsibility was not to enforce policy but to defend true religion. The implication was clear: The Contra-Remonstrants were the orthodox party in the dispute. Maurits's support emboldened the Contra-Remonstrants. On July 19, 1617, they broke into the Cloister Church (*Kloosterkerk*) in The Hague and began holding worship services there in clear violation of the edicts passed by the States of Holland. On July 23, Maurits himself joined them to worship in the Cloister Church.

Led by Advocate General Oldenbarnevelt, the States of Holland took decisive action, passing on August 4 the "Sharp Resolution" (*Scherpe Resolutie*). The province of Holland had formally called in May for a national synod to resolve the religious dispute, but the resolution asserted that no provincial government had the power to convene a national synod. That power resided solely with the national government of the States. Furthermore, the resolution provided for the raising of a national guard (*waardgelders*) to maintain order in the municipalities and enforce national law. In effect this set up a power struggle between the advocate general, Oldenbarnevelt, and Prince Maurits. The country was literally on the brink of civil war. The national guard was being raised in cities led by Remonstrant councils, so Prince Maurits began a process of dismantling the city councils, first dismissing Remonstrant council members and then appointing all Contra-Remonstrant councils. At this point, all support for Advocate General Oldenbarnevelt evaporated. He was arrested on August 29, 1618. After being tried on trumped-up charges of treason, he was condemned as a traitor, and on May 13, 1619, the former advocate general was beheaded.

His arrest in late August paved the way for the Synod of Dort to convene in November 1618. This brings us finally to the point of this history lesson. In the months leading up to the Dort Synod, a book appeared that was evidently read by almost every delegate to the Synod, *Specimen controversiarum Belgicarum*. The author was Arminius's long-time ecclesial adversary, Festus Hommius. The book caricatures Arminius's theological anthropology as overly optimistic regarding human capacities: Human beings are "not slaves of sin, but free to will good and evil."[13] This type of caricature had been playing out for a decade in the pamphlet and civil warfare that we have noted. The actual theology of Arminius was by this point almost completely lost beyond the horizon of struggles for political dominance.

Aza Goudriaan has pointed out that these assertions do not "fit especially well into the text of Articles three and four of the Remonstrance of 1610, which insists that the human being cannot 'think, will or do anything that is good' except by the grace of God."[14] This theological anthropology is taken directly from Arminius's 1608 *Declaration of Sentiments*. Excepting their appearance in caricature as scapegoats in the rhetorical warfare, Arminius's actual teachings had already to a large extent been lost from sight by the time the Synod of Dort convened. Most notably missing was the seriousness with which Arminius took Augustinian teachings on fallen humanity and humanity's utter inability to make a contribution in any way to God's saving initiative in Christ.

This slow disappearing act was accelerated by Arminius's own student, Simon Episcopius, who was the leading spokesman for the Remonstrants at the Synod of Dort, as well as by Arminius's life-long friend, Peter Bertius.[15] If the Contra-Remonstrants at Dort closed the coffin on Arminius, the Remonstrants themselves lowered him into the ground and covered him over with Pelagian sentiment. Even as we contemplate the more recent absence of Arminius in Wesleyan-Arminian theology, history teaches us that Arminius's theology was already much obscured roughly a century prior to Wesley's birth.

ARMINIUS THE ANGLICAN: CAMBRIDGE PLATONIST AND LATITUDINARIAN DILUTIONS

Despite proto-Arminian tendencies in some quarters of the Church of England, a case may be made that it was through the Synod of Dort that Arminianism became widely known in England. King James I sent no fewer than eight different persons as official delegates to the Synod of Dort. The delegation did not go to Holland particularly inclined in favor of Arminianism, and due to the harsh handling the Arminians received, the delegates were actually less opposed to Arminianism upon their return. The famous Arminian Hugo Grotius visited England in 1613 and his friendship with Bishop Lancelot Andrewes "ripened theology's coming into a long correspondence on subjects both ecclesiastical and political."[16]

Slowly but surely, through Latitudinarian sentiment and especially by way of Cambridge Platonism, Arminianism penetrated the Church of England. Here an important qualification is in order. It was the Latitudinarian concept of a tolerant, nonjudging God that carried the day, not Arminius's theology itself. Arminius's distinctive emphases were by now totally obscure, notwithstanding Tobias Conyers's translation of his *Declaration of Sentiments* under the title, *The Just Man's Defence*, in 1657. England apparently imbibed the optimistic anthropology of Episcopius's Arminianism more than the Augustinian/Calvinist anthropology of Arminius. This does, in fact, provide us a clue with regard to why Wesley's Arminianism was rather different than most English Arminianism.

In ecclesial offices and in university halls, the spirit of the age was increasingly inclined to the moderate sensibilities of Erasmus. Like him, the Cambridge Platonists relied principally upon the authority of Scripture for their truth: "They sought the "root" of Christianity...not as their own exclusive property or their particular password to heaven but as the strong essence of faith that might draw together into one communion all Christendom—or at least all Protestant Christendom."[17] They had the scholar's approach to be sure, but they were in their origins rather on the conservative side of the scale. In other words, they wished to conserve the best that the historic Christian faith had bequeathed to posterity. To do this, they believed that the ancient articles of faith must be put to the scrutiny of reason, and they were sincere in their belief that the Christian reasoning would turn the mind to fraternal love and God's honor. Rosalie Colie has appropriately observed, "The Cambridge Platonists sought to save as much of life for men as could be saved, to open men's mind to the love of God, to divest men of their fear of a vengeful Jehovah, so that all men might pass their lives quietly and properly in the pursuit of their callings and in the worship of God."[18] Their fear of religious enthusiasm, however, led them to rely increasingly so much on pure rationality that they—certainly not on purpose—paved the way for deism. However, the Cambridge Platonists can no more be held responsible for deism than can the Cartesian "hermeneutic of suspicion" that so fully came to characterize the modern Enlightenment.

Even so, it is clear that the kindred spirits of English Arminianism and Cambridge Platonism were mirrors of the age, even if

Arminius would have himself been loath to see his reflection there. One of Arminius's theological heirs, Philippus van Limborch, minister in Amsterdam and professor there at the Remonstrant seminary, carried on for two decades (1667–1687) a correspondence with Henry More and Ralph Cudworth that reveals a genuine connection between the aims of the Platonists in England and the Arminians in Holland—"a closeness of purpose indicative of an astonishingly similar moral attitude and outlook on the spiritual and physical worlds."[19] Limborch was also a kindred spirit and close acquaintance of John Locke, with whom he carried on an active correspondence from 1685 to 1704, the year of Locke's death in Amsterdam where he had lived in exile among the tolerant Dutch for 20 years.[20]

Whereas in Holland the Arminian Remonstrants were driven out of the land, rather the reverse proved to be the case in England. At the risk of oversimplification, it can be said that the Arminian prelates of the Church of England were generally the persecutors: "Archbishop Laud's insistence upon conformity drove the Puritan factions within the Church first out of it and then to join with Presbyterians and Independents in open revolt."[21] In the Cromwellian era, Laud, like Oldenbarnevelt, died on the scaffold, although for different reasons. Also, like Oldenbarnevelt, Laud died convinced that he was right both religiously and politically. But after the Cromwellian revolt, the reconstructed Church became increasingly Arminian. This was so much the case that, by 1688, "the technical triumph of Arminianism in [Anglican] England was complete."[22] George Morley's jesting reply to the question of "What do the Arminians hold?"—"All the best bishoprics and deaneries in England!"—was more accurate than the uninitiated would anticipate.[23]

To be sure, English Arminianism was not confined to the established Church of England. Such independents as John Goodwin, for example, defended Arminianism against Presbyterianism. Henry Hammond's Arminian-inclined annotations on the Bible were to stand in place of the Genevan annotations, still influential in many quarters. It is not a great exaggeration to assert that Arminianism of the Latitudinarian sort penetrated church life everywhere in England, except among the staunch Presbyterians, true Calvinists almost to a man.

ARMINIUS THE WESLEYAN: JOHN WESLEY'S PARTIAL AND POLEMICAL RECOVERY

Such was the Arminian-inclined Church of England into which John and Charles Wesley were born. It is clear that neither Arminius as an important persona, nor his distinctive theological emphases, played a significant role in English Arminianism to this point. This is not to say, however, that he was unknown. In 1715, Thomas Bennet published *Directions for Studying*, in which Arminius's distinctive soteriological emphases are cited at length. Richard Heitzenrater informs us that John Wesley bought a copy of this book in late 1730 and read it through in January 1731.[24] This reading included the reproduction of Arminius's concise summary of four divine decrees related to predestination as found in the *Declaration of Sentiments* (which served as the foundation for the Remonstrance of 1610), as well as the full text of *Public Disputation* 15 (on Divine Predestination).[25]

An earlier essay explores the common soteriological distinctives in greater depth and detail than is possible here.[26] Suffice it to say that Wesley was aware and made conscious appropriation of Arminius's very specific highlighting of these points:

1. Salvation is located solely in the person and work of Christ as Redeemer.
2. All who by grace believe will be saved, and those who do not believe will be damned.
3. God through Christ provides the grace to believe.

What Wesley tends to avoid in his soteriology, with the notable exception of select tracts on predestination, is the issue of divine knowledge regarding those who will not believe and who therefore will be damned. Indeed, Arminius himself tried very hard to avoid this speculative piece, but his opponents simply would not allow him to do so.

Following Carl Bangs, Gerritt Jan Hoenderdaal has asserted that Wesley probably did not understand Arminius well. Hendrikus Berkhof has asserted that of all the Wesleyans who take soteriology seriously, the evangelical/Holiness tradition Wesleyans are the most likely to have inherited the "true ring" of Arminius.

With regard to his covenant and decree emphases, in fact, Wesley probably did not understand Arminius well. Evidence is lacking as to whether Wesley read extensively enough in Arminius to have been aware of what Arminius actually taught in these areas. However, as noted in Gunter's essay cited earlier, Wesley was very much on the same page with Arminius with regard to how divine prevenient grace preserves the three emphases noted above. There is a remarkable parallel in the distinctive way that prevenience is appropriated in Wesley. It is almost as if Wesley were copying from the theological progression in Arminius's *Declaration of Sentiments*. Yet, direct literary dependence is not apparent, hence the qualification that Wesley only *partially* recovered the distinctive emphases of Arminius. This Arminian emphasis is rooted in Augustinian anthropological assumptions requiring an evangelical doctrine of prevenient grace that proactively enables sinful humans to respond positively to God's salvific overtures.

In Wesley's teaching sermons as well as in his occasional theological tracts, a consistent Arminian soteriology can be observed from 1730 until the early 1770s, but at this juncture a controversy arises in which these distinctives are blurred. The blurred distinctions do not come directly from Wesley's hand, but they do arise at the annual conference overseen by him, for the Minutes of which he was accountable. It appears that the unguarded phrasing in the 1770 Minutes reflects Pelagian tendencies into which Methodist movements have been continually inclined to fall. Just as in Wesley's era, formal theological pronouncements emphasize the sinfulness of lost humanity and the absolute need for divine grace for salvation, but the insistence of using an expression like "free will" leads invariably down a Pelagian blind alley where human initiative and ability implicitly trump divine grace.

In the late 1760s and early 1770s, the Wesleyan Methodist revival was at a high tide that some felt was beginning to ebb, and there was evidently a felt need to distinguish the Wesleyan wave from the tide of Whitefield's and the Calvinist Methodists' effective evangelistic efforts. Whatever took place at the annual conference of Wesleyan Methodist preachers in 1770, the Minutes of Conference read as follows:[27]

Q. We said in 1744, "We have leaned too much toward Calvinism." Wherein?

A. (1) With regard to man's faithfulness. Our Lord himself taught us to use the expression: Therefore we ought never to be ashamed of it. We ought steadily to assert upon his authority, that if a man is not "faithful in the unrighteous mammon, God will not give him the true riches."

(2) With regard to "working for life," which our Lord expressly commands us to do. "Labour," *ergazethe*, literally, "work, for the meat that endureth to everlasting life." And in fact, every believer, till he comes to glory, works for as well as from life.

(3) We have received it as a maxim, that "a man is to do nothing in order to justification." Nothing can be more false. Whoever desires to find favour with God, should "cease from evil, and learn to do well."...Whoever repents, should "do works meet for repentance." And if this is not in order to find favour, what does he do them for?

Once more review the whole affair:...

(4) Is not this salvation by works?

Not by the merit of works, but by works as a condition.

(5) What have we then been disputing about for these thirty years?

I am afraid about words....

(6) As to merit itself, of which we have been so dreadfully afraid: We are rewarded according to our works, yea, because of our works. How does this differ from, "for the sake of our works?" And how differs this from *secundum merita operam* which is not more than, "as our works deserve." Can you split this hair? I doubt, I cannot.

These statements inclined more in the direction of Pelagian moralism than perhaps anything Wesley had ever preached or published. In May of 1771, the *Gospel-Magazine* published the section on works from the Methodist *Minutes*, labeling them as "Popery unmasked."[28] Contrast these moralistic recordings to Wesley's theological writings at the earliest beginnings of the movement, especially his *Scripture Doctrine Concerning Predestination* in 1741.[29] Although the tract was only sixteen (3 x 5 inches) pages in its first edition, it is a consistent piece of Arminian interpretation of Ephesians 1:4, 1 Peter 1:2, and 2 Thessalonians 2:13-14. As is implied in the title, Wesley's primary concern in this brief tract is to describe the scriptural foundation underlying his contention that election is founded in divine foreknowledge and that election is for the purpose of sanctification to good works. His overarching purpose in both of these goals, however, is to free the doctrine of predestination from its captivity to speculative theologizing. His point of departure is 1 Peter 1:2: "Elect, according to the Foreknowledge of God, thro' Sanctification of the Spirit, unto Obedience." If the elect are chosen through sanctification of the Holy Spirit,

> then they were not chosen before they were sanctify'd by the Spirit. But they were not sanctify'd by the Spirit, before they had a Being. It is plain then, neither were they chosen from the Foundation of the world. But "God calleth Things that are not, as tho' they were."

He also applies this Arminian exegesis to 2 Thessalonians 2:13:

> God hath from the beginning chosen you to Salvation, thro' Sanctification of the spirit, and Belief of the Truth, and called to believe it by the Gospel. Therefore they were not chosen before they believed; much less before they had a Being, any more than Christ was slain, before *he* had a Being.[30]

Wesley believed that the Bible is clear about what predestination implies:

> It is God's fore-appointing obedient Believers to Salvation, not without, but "according to his Foreknowledge" of all their Works, "from the Foundation of the World." And so likewise he predestinates or fore-appoints all disobedient Unbelievers to Damnation, not without, but "according to his foreknowledge" of all their Works, "from the Foundation of the World."[31]

A significant portion of the rest of the tract describes the basis for the universality of the gospel, and Wesley concluded by asserting that he taught that humans had, not a free will, but a "freed will" by which they could graciously respond to the universal proclamation: "Man hath his Freedom of Will, not naturally, but by Grace."[32]

ARMINIUS THE PELAGIAN: JOHN FLETCHER AND METHODIST POLEMICAL THEOLOGY

In the aftermath of the initial Minutes controversy, John Fletcher became the primary theological voice that engaged the Calvinist protégés of Whitefield. In Fletcher's *Checks to Antinomianism*, there is a sustained line of argumentation around the issue of good works on the part of believers and how these works relate to the gift of salvation. Clearly, the apologetic is that good works play a "secondary" rather than a primary, causative role in salvation. What the early Methodists, and Methodists since then, seem to have missed is that this actually constitutes a potentially momentous theological shift from theocentricity to anthropocentricity.

In nineteenth-century Methodism, preachers in training were required to read Fletcher's *Checks to Antinomianism* as a guard against falling into predestination, but apparently they were not required to read Wesley's more Arminius-inclined and theologically nuanced *Scripture Doctrine Concerning Predestination* and *Predestination Calmly Considered* or other related tracts. The Wesleyan homilies that were required reading simply do not deal with these subtle theological points. As Randy Maddox has pointed out, "Wesley bequeathed to his movement a [few essays that reflected not only] the core of the Christian theological heritage (with certain characteristic doctrinal emphases), but [more especially] a multi-level model of the 'practical theologian.'"[33]

Sources from the formational period of nineteenth-century Methodism reflect that only theological tracts in the *Book of Discipline*, Wesley's *Sermons*, and his *Notes upon the New Testament* comprised the bulk of theological reading. Even where reference is made in the sources to reading these, there are more entries that reflect little or no reading of *any* theological tracts. In the process of American Methodism's distinguishing itself, recourse was rather consistently taken to Fletcher's *Checks to Antinomianism*. Maddox concludes, "As such it became common from the first generation for American preachers to equate Methodist theology with Wesley's *Sermons* and Fletcher's *Checks*."[34] Maddox is correct to point out that Fletcher develops an extended apologetic on cooperant grace, entire sanctification, and the universal offer of salvation, or "general redemption" as distinguished from "particular election." For our purposes, Maddox's insight is helpful when he notes that "early American Methodists gravitated toward Fletcher's rigorous apologetics as their standard model."[35]

American Methodism also adopted substantial content and theological assumptions from Fletcher—who spilt a gallon of ink on hundreds of pages related to gospel dispensation and the secondary, nonmeritorious role of good works in the present saving dispensation. An unintended consequence of Fletcher's emphases carried to their logical conclusion was an anthropocentric shift in Methodist soteriology. The perceived theological importance of Fletcher's method and content carries well into the twentieth century. As an aspiring young theologian, I was quite strongly urged by one of my mentors to "absorb" Fletcher's *Checks*. In the decades prior to our rediscovery of Wesley—reflected in the decision to publish a critical edition of his works, initiate the Wesleyan studies group in the American Academy of Religion, and found Kingswood Books—more than a few doctoral dissertations examined Fletcher's thought as a way to understand Methodist distinctives: the Nazarene John A. Knight and Methodists David Shipley and Al Coppedge among them, to name only a prominent few.

This is not a historical accident, but rather the partial result of a consequential chain of events set off by Wesley and Fletcher themselves. The Minutes controversy of 1770 actually became known as the Antinomian Controversy, hence Fletcher's multivolume *Checks to Antinomianism*. In the heated pamphlet warfare that carried on for several years between the warring Arminian and Calvinist factions of English evangelicals, the Wesleyan-Arminian faction was reduced to being Pelagian and the Calvinist evangelicals were caricatured as antinomians. At the end of this pamphleteering, Wesley initiated a distinctive periodical under the title *The Arminian Magazine* to distinguish his Methodist movement. His reasons for doing this are explicitly stated in volume one: to respond to publications such as *The Spiritual Magazine* and *Gospel-Magazine* that espoused limited atonement, defending the belief that God's will is for all to be saved.[36] Each issue would contain (1) a theological defense, (2) an extract from the life of a holy person, (3) accounts and letters from pious persons, and (4) an exposition of relevant Scripture verses or passages.

In short, *The Arminian Magazine* was pure polemic. Wesley was true to his promise to publish biographical vignettes in every monthly installment, and he began with Luther. But on Calvin he did not publish an overview of Calvin's godly life. Instead he reproduced a summary of Calvin's harsh treatment of those who disagreed with him theologically, specifically Michael Servetus and Sebastian Castellio (May 1778).[37] Castellio's *Dialogues* on predestination, election, and free will were reproduced extensively from

January of 1781 to September of 1782.³⁸ As chief editor, Wesley also selected treatises from the English Arminians Thomas Goad, John Plaifere, and John Goodwin for publication. Here the point was specifically and pointedly made that supralapsarian Calvinism makes God the author of sin—a conclusion that Arminius himself also draws in his *Declaration of Sentiments*. Wesley also republished his own *Predestination Calmly Considered*. In the installment for November of 1779,³⁹ Wesley emphasized a distinctive Arminian note, that in the act of salvation, God does everything—human beings have only the power to resist.⁴⁰ Arminius would agree. It is difficult to harmonize this insight with Fletcher's preoccupation with the role that works play in our salvation—albeit a secondary, noncausative role. Arminius's dialectic (and Wesley's also in this essay) is decidedly different from Fletcher's. The Arminian dialectic was further lost from view in subsequent developments among Wesley's heirs.

Through the nineteenth and until the middle part of the twentieth century, John Wesley functioned as the chief founder-preacher of Methodism, but Fletcher was viewed as the chief theologian. Wesley was simply not taken seriously as a theological mentor. And Fletcher's situated polemics assured that he had mostly unkind things to say about the thought of his Calvinist "opponents." Indeed, his apologetic is at times a reminder of overstatement akin to Augustine versus Pelagius, except that the door Fletcher unintentionally seems to have left open is the back door of Pelagian anthropocentricity. It is not that Fletcher was weak on *sin*, it is rather the case that he was preoccupied with the contribution that human works play in salvation. It is this emphasis in American Methodism and Wesleyan Christianity that is so utterly contrary to Arminius's theological sentiments.

Even in the decades prior to 1980 when it was not unusual to hear the phrase "Wesleyan-Arminian theology," it was a truncated Arminius in the theological algorithm. Carl Bangs and his sister, Mildred Bangs Wynkoop, may have been the only ones keenly aware that Arminius also had some things to say about what is touted as a Wesleyan distinctive—sanctification and perfection. Wesley himself probably did not know this either! Wesleyans have self-identified as Arminians by affirming the universal offer of salvation that all might be saved, even if not all *would* be. But Wesleyans have also equated the Arminian tradition with total opposition to notions of predestination.

The problem is that Arminius would not have felt comfortable at all with sweeping categorical assertions against predestination. Arminius believed quite strongly in predestination. Even as he would stand with Wesleyans for the doctrine of evangelical prevenience, Arminius would not share the preoccupation with the role of works in "working out our salvation." If we are lost, it will be our own damning fault; but when we believe, it will be by grace alone. Works have nothing to do with it. Ultimately, Arminius would call Wesleyans back to an Augustinian emphasis on the saving initiative of our sovereign God who has in Christ made covenant to save lost humanity. If Wesleyans can recover Arminius's sense of the love-centered sovereignty of God, then it might actually be possible to speak with some degree of accuracy of a Wesleyan-Arminian theology.

NOTES

1. For the first English translation of the original Dutch text and its background, see Gunter.

2. This essay is being written parallel to an essay, "The Transformation of Arminianism from the Death of Arminius to the Synod of Dort, 1609–1619," that will appear in Robert Webster, ed., *Perfecting Perfection: Studies in Honor of Henry D. Rack* (Eugene, Oreg.: Pickwick Publications, forthcoming). The opening pages of this essay repeat some of that material relating to the loss of Arminius's theological emphases among the Remonstrants.

3. "Calvinist" in this context is admittedly anachronistic, since Calvin was seen as one of many leading Reformed theologians and was himself a highly significant influence on Arminius.

4. Douglas Nobbs, *Theocracy and Toleration: A Study of the Disputes in Dutch Calvinism from 1600–1650* (Cambridge: University Press, 1938), 25–212.

5. Michael Adam Hakkenberg, "The Predestinarian Controversy in the Netherlands, 1600–1620" (Ph.D. diss., University of California, Berkeley, 1989), 4.

6. Cf. Alastair Duke, "The Ambivalent Face of Calvinism in the Netherlands, 1561–1618," in *International Calvinism, 1541–1715*, ed. Menna Prestwich (Oxford: Clarendon Press, 1985), 109.

7. Cf. Gunter, esp. 135–36, 180, 190–91.

8. Pieter Geyl, *The Netherlands Divided (1609–1648)*, trans. S. T. Bindoff (London: Williams and Norgate, 1936), 52.

9. Jan Den Tex, *Oldenbarnevelt*, trans. R. B. Powell (Cambridge: University Press, 1973) 2:554.

10. Ibid., 2:680.

11. Quoted in ibid., 2:566.

12. Hakkenberg, "The Predestinarian Controversy," 48, quoting Peter Blok, *History of the People of the Netherlands*, trans. Ruth Putnam (New York: G. P. Putnam's Sons, 1900), 3:438–39.

13. Festus Hommius, *Specimen controversiarum Belgicarum* (ex Office Elzeviriana, 1618).

14. Aza Goudriaan, "The Synod of Dordt on Arminian Anthropology," in *Revisiting the Synod of Dordt, 1618–1619*, ed. A. Goudriaan (Leiden: Brill, 2011), 82.

15. See Gunter's forthcoming chapter, "The Transformation of Arminianism."

16. Rosalie Colie, *Light and Enlightenment: A Study of the Cambridge Platonists and the Dutch Arminians* (Cambridge: University Press, 1957), 15. To my mind there is still not a better study of Latitudinarian Arminianism in England than Colie's.

17. Ibid., 2.

18. Ibid., 3.

19. Ibid., 7. See also Nobbs, *Theocracy and Toleration*.

20. See the online archives of the University of Amsterdam for this correspondence.

21. Colie, *Light and Enlightenment*, 21.

22. Robert S. Bosher, *The Making of the Restoration Settlement* (London: Dacre, 1951), cited by Colie, *Light and Enlightenment*, 21.

23. Carl Bangs, "'All the Best Bishoprics and Deaneries': The Enigma of Arminian Politics," *Church History* 42, no. 1 (1973): 5–12.

24. Richard P. Heitzenrater, *John Wesley and the Oxford Methodists, 1725–35* (Ph.D. diss., Duke University, 1972), 351n1.

25. Thomas Bennet, *Directions for Studying*, 3d ed. (London: James and John Knapton, 1727), 95–99. The quotation is from the Latin text of the *Declaration* found in *Opera*, 119. The text of *Disp. pub.*, XV comes from *Opera*, 283–85. On p. 99, Bennet also refers the reader to *Disp. priv.*, XL–XLIII, lamenting that their length prohibited copying them within this book.

26. For a more involved argument for Wesley's soteriological fidelity to Arminius, see W. Stephen Gunter, "John Wesley, a Faithful Representative of Jacob Arminius," *Wesleyan Theological Journal* 42, no. 2 (2007): 65–82.

27. John Wesley, *Minutes of the Methodist Conference* (1770), in *The Bicentennial Edition of the Works of John Wesley*, vol. 10, *The Methodist Societies: The Minutes of Conference*, ed. Henry D. Rack (Nashville: Abingdon Press, 2011).

28. *The Gospel-Magazine* 65 (May 1771): 230–32. Cf. W. Stephen Gunter, *Limits of Love Divine* (Nashville: Kingswood Books, 1989), 227–66.

29. John Wesley, *The Scripture Doctrine Concerning Predestination*,

Election, and Reprobation: Extracted from a Late Author [W. Haggar?] (London: Strahan, 1741). Wesley included this in his work, *A Preservative against Unsettled Notions* (Bristol: E. Farley, 1758), 177–92. He republished it in *AM* 2 (1779): 105–12. It also appeared in Benson's edition of the *The Works of the Rev. John Wesley* (London, 1812), 14:382–96.

30. Randy Maddox, "Respected Founder/Neglected Guide: The Role of Wesley in American Methodist Theology," *Methodist History* 37 (1999): 72.

31. Wesley, *The Scripture Doctrine Concerning Predestination*, in Benson, *The Works of the Rev. John Wesley*, 14:421.

32. Ibid., 422.

33. Ibid., 429.

34. Maddox, "Respected Founder/Neglected Guide," 75.

35. Ibid., 76.

36. *AM* 1 (1778): iii–viii.

37. Ibid., 201–9. The summary is taken from Samuel Chandler, *The History of Persecution from the Patriarchal Age to the Reign of George II* (London: J. Gray, 1736).

38. *AM* 4 (1781): 7–15, 65–72, 121–28, 177–84, 233–38, 289–94, 345–52, 401–8, 457–63, 513–19, 569–74, 625–30; *AM* 5 (1782): 1–7, 57–61, 113–17, 169–73, 225–30, 281–85, 337–41, 339–97, 449–52.

39. *AM* 2:553–80.

40. W. Stephen Gunter, *An Annotated Content Index:* The Arminian Magazine, *Vols. 1–20 (1778–1797)*, 41, accessed June 27, 2013, http://divinity.duke.edu/sites/divinity.duke.edu/files/documents/cswt/Arminian_Magazine_vols_1–20.pdf.

CHAPTER 5

JACOB ARMINIUS AND JONATHAN EDWARDS ON THE DOCTRINE OF CREATION

Oliver D. Crisp

"He suffered much at the hands of his interpreters."[1] This literary proverb could very easily be applied to Jacob Arminius. As Keith Stanglin has put it, the trouble is no one "owns" Arminius; he has no "tribe" as do Luther or Calvin or Cranmer. Lutherans love Luther; the Reformed (by and large) look to Calvin; Anglicans regard Cranmer as their English Reformer. But Arminius is the common property of many who claim his name as their rallying cry and some who are not even clear about what Arminianism entails. Wesleyans are Arminians of a sort. But then so are Dutch Remonstrants and general Baptists and Anabaptists, as are many evangelicals of no particular confession.

What is more, the Harmenszoon of history is not the same as the Arminius of faith. The Arminius of faith undermined Reformed orthodoxy, creating schism in the church by teaching a synergistic doctrine of salvation and denying God's absolute sovereignty in creation and redemption. He tended toward a semi-Pelagian account of human beings postfall, made election conditional upon foreseen faith, entertained the notion that the atonement is universal in scope, thought grace was resistible, and doubted that one's election was sure and certain. The Harmenszoon of history is a rather more complex character. He is a biblical theologian, one for whom Scripture is the principal norm for all matters of Christian doctrine. Yet he was also a scholastic theologian, who used the elenctic and disputatious methods of school theology, harnessing them to Ramist logic and a penchant for the doctrine of God's middle knowledge, which he may have introduced to Protestant thought. He was also a Reformed minister and latterly professor, even if the substance of his doctrine did not comport in every respect with the mainstream of that tradition and might even be thought antithetical to it in some important respects.[2] Add to the question of the reception of Arminius's thought and his place in the history of Christian theology the problems associated with his writings, not all of which are in the public domain and most of which are not in a modern critical edition. It seems amazing to think that the nearest thing to an English translation of the works of a theologian of such influence and importance was last attempted in the nineteenth century as a labor of love.[3]

The Amsterdam Oude Kerk, where Arminius served as minister from 1588 to 1603. Courtesy of The Leiden American Pilgrim Museum.

The focus of this chapter is the doctrine of creation proper. This doctrine overlaps with several others in much traditional theology, including the doctrines of election, or providence. But in this chapter, we shall concern ourselves with the doctrine of creation, not with election and providence as they bear upon creation, though these are important, and controversial, matters in Arminius's thought. The occasion of this piece was the publication of the first introductory work to Arminius's theology for some time in the volume *Jacob Arminius: Theologian of Grace*, coauthored by Keith Stanglin and Thomas McCall.[4] There the authors draw attention to the shape and orthodoxy of Arminius's understanding of creation and to the fact that Arminius has often been misinterpreted and misunderstood on this topic as on several others. In order to test Stanglin and McCall's thesis that the Arminius of faith is a rather different theologian from the Harmenszoon of history, I will compare Arminius's doctrine with a Reformed thinker of the eighteenth century often regarded in contemporary popular evangelicalism as a paradigm of Reformed thought, Jonathan Edwards.

Despite the distance in time and geography that separates Arminius from Edwards, the comparison is instructive. Contemporary evangelicals usually regard Edwards as an exemplar of Reformed theology. For the "young, restless, and Reformed" constituency, Edwards is a poster boy, whose theology epitomizes what Reformed theology ought to look like, over and against the perceived anthropocentric theology of Arminianism.[5] In the influential popularizing works of ministers like John Piper, Edwards is lionized for his emphasis upon absolute divine sovereignty and divine self-glorification in the creation of the world.[6] However, we shall see that of the two divines it is Edwards whose doctrine presses at the bounds of what is theologically permissible whilst Arminius's doctrine is well within the parameters of orthodoxy, even if untypical of Reformed theology in several respects.

ARMINIUS ON GOD AND CREATION

In his important study of Arminius's doctrines of God, creation, and providence, Richard Muller remarks, "It is apparent not only that Arminius' doctrine of creation, like his doctrine of God, is profoundly indebted to the scholastic tradition, particularly to the tradition of Thomism, but also that his doctrine of creation is one of the fundamental pivots of his theological system."[7] The doctrine of creation was not peripheral or unimportant to Arminius's system;

it occupies a foundational place and is connected to several other loci that are of considerable importance for rightly understanding the shape of his work, particularly (as already indicated) his understanding of election and providence. For this reason, it behooves us to pay careful attention to the form his doctrine takes.

To understand rightly the shape of Arminius's view it is necessary to begin with aspects of his doctrine of God, for like most traditional dogmatic accounts of creation, the work of God *ad extra* is intimately related to the nature of God as God relates to creation. Arminius endorsed a traditional, classical account of the divine nature according to which God is a simple pure act. He says this of God's simplicity:

> Simplicity is a pre-eminent mode of the Essence of God, by which it is void of all composition, and of component parts, whether they belong to the senses or the understanding. He is without composition, because without external cause; and he is without component parts because without internal cause.... The essence of God therefore neither consists of material, integral, and quantitive parts, of matter and form, of kind and difference, of subject and accident, nor of form and the thing formed...neither hypothetically and through nature, through capability and actuality, nor through essence and being. Hence God is his own Essence and his own Being.[8]

In keeping with much late medieval and Protestant orthodox theology, Arminius is clear that the essence of God "is that by which God exists."[9] The life of God is, he says, "an Act flowing from the Essence of God, by which his Essence is signified to be [*actuosa*] in action itself."[10] Moreover, the life of God "is the Essence itself, and his very Being; because the divine Essence is in every respect simple, as well as infinite, and therefore eternal and immutable."[11] His views in this regard remain consistent across his public and private disputations. Even on a cursory reading of the relevant sections of his works it is clear that he does not substantially deviate from the norms of western catholicism regarding the divine nature or the divine life. Thus, in his *Private Disputations* he writes, "This Essence is free from all composition, so it cannot enter into the composition of any thing."[12] Moreover, "The life of God...is most simple, so that it is not, in reality, distinguished from his essence" so that "according to the confined capacity of our conception, by which it is distinguished from his essence, it may, in some degree, be described as being 'an act that flows from the essence of God,' by which is intimated that it is active in itself."[13] We cannot know the divine essence, he avers. But we can apprehend some things dimly, and by analogy, about God and about God's life. In this manner, we are able to see that being essentially noncomposite and being essentially in act are both predicates that apply to the divine essence.

Stanglin and McCall point out that this endorsement of divine simplicity in Arminius may be more Scotist than Thomist.[14] Thomas Aquinas allowed that there are "rational" or purely conceptual distinctions that can be predicated of God, so that we can speak of the distinct divine persons of the Godhead. But he denied that there are "real" distinctions in God as there are between, say, the parts of creaturely bodies, because God's nature is simple. However, Scotus added to this the idea that there are "formal" distinctions in God, where a formal distinction picks out some differentiation within the essence of a thing. Thus, the color and texture of an apple are formally distinct, but belong numerically to the same entity. Arminius echoes this Scotist language at one point in his *Public Disputations*, where, during a discussion of divine simplicity, he remarks that "whatever is absolutely predicated about God, it is to be understood essentially and not accidentally; and those things (whether many or diverse) which are predicated concerning God, are, in God, not many but one.... It is only in our mode of considering them, which is a compound mode, that they are distinguished as being many and diverse." He continues, "though this may not inappropriately, be said—because they are likewise distinguished by a formal reason."[15]

From simplicity conjoined with divine infinity, Arminius derives divine eternity (i.e., atemporality), immensity, immutability, impassibility, and incorruptibility. These are all incommunicable attributes—that is, divine perfections that God does not share in common with creatures.[16] Out of this perfect, singular life God creates the world ex nihilo.[17] Creation is the product of his communicable attributes, including divine goodness, wisdom, will, and power.[18] More specifically, it is the contingent output of the intrinsic self-diffusiveness of divine goodness, in which all creatures participate. As Muller points out, this aspect of Arminius's doctrine is thoroughly Thomist in nature and underlines the connection between the classical understanding of the divine nature and what it is that leads to the creation.[19] God wills to create a world in which creatures may participate in God's goodness. However, this is a free act of God; nothing impels God to act in this fashion, not even something intrinsic to the divine nature. For, says Arminius, "the Lord Omnipotent did not create the world by a natural necessity, but by the freedom of his will."[20] (We shall see that by modifying this essentially Thomist component of a classical doctrine of God, Edwards ends up with a very different understanding of God's freedom in creation.)

Yet as Arminius understands divine aseity and freedom this means God is free to refrain from creating and has no need of the created order. God's blessedness (*beatitas*) is perfect delight in God's own perfection.[21] This is an incommunicable attribute peculiar to God that is both an act of understanding and will, and the fount of blessing to the creature. But God does not need to create; there is nothing in the divine nature that requires an act of creation to manifest this blessedness or bring about the instantiation of the divine glory *ad extra*. As Stanglin and McCall put it, "Arminius insists that the simplicity and aseity of God imply that God lacks nothing good—thus the external display of the divine glory is not necessary for God."[22] Moreover, "God can lack nothing and can have no need—not even the need for glorification through the display of justice or wrath."[23] As Arminius has it, "God...does not need to illustrate his glory extrinsically, by mercy and justice or wrath, nor by grace, as it is here understood. But God can make use of the sinner for the glory of his grace, mercy, wrath, or severity, if he sees fit to do so (*visum fuerit*)."[24]

There are other aspects to his doctrine of creation that are relevant to our present concern. For instance, Arminius denies that God could create creatures purely for the purposes of destroying them in hell. Instead, God creates according to God's essentially benevolent nature, so that all God brings into existence is good.[25] What God wills to create, God creates *per se*, or in itself, as good. Evil is not willed *per se*, but *per accidens*—that is, accidentally, or contingently, not as an expression of the essential goodness of God.[26] This reflects the fact that Arminius is an intellectualist, not a voluntarist. That is, he thinks God creates for good reasons that are logically and explanatorily prior to that which he wills. By contrast, the voluntarist says that there are no such antecedent reasons that guide God's actions *ad extra*. Thus in his *Declaration of Sentiments*, Arminius writes,

Rather than being alien to God, creation is an act quite proper to him. It is eminently an action most appropriate to him. It is an act to which he could be moved by no other external cause. Indeed, it is the primordial act of God, and until it was completed, nothing could have any actual existence except God himself. For everything else that has being came into existence through this act.[27]

Although the topic here is not providence proper, some remarks about Arminius's understanding of the act of creation as it bears upon the divine governance of the world are appropriate at this juncture. For one thing, Arminius does not appear to endorse the scholastic doctrine of continuous creation. On this view both the act of creation and the sustenance of that which is created thereafter are two aspects of one eternal timeless divine act, apprehended as distinct events in time by finite human creatures. By contrast, Arminius appears to think these two things are distinct divine actions and (somewhat strangely) that God brings them about in time: "It is an act of the practical understanding, or of the will employing the understanding, not completed in a single moment, but continued in the moments of the duration of things."[28] It is difficult to see what can be meant by the claim that a timeless, simple pure act (somehow) brings about different actions in time, because such a being can have no temporal relations. It is easier, I think, to see what might be meant by the claim that the one, eternal, simple, pure act that is God brings about distinct temporal effects: creation with time and the conservation of creation thereafter. However, this does not appear to be what Arminius actually says. At least one recent interpreter of Arminius thinks we should take this at face value as a claim about temporal divine actions, which raises a concern about the integrity of Arminius's theology.[29]

Arminius is also a defender of Molinism—that is, the doctrine of divine middle knowledge. In this respect, he was unusual among the Reformed of the period of early Reformed orthodoxy spanning the second half of the sixteenth century and into the early decades of the seventeenth century. Although he does not name Luis de Molina, it is clear from a number of places that he endorsed the doctrine.[30] All parties agreed that God has natural knowledge (i.e., knowledge of all that is necessary and possible) and free knowledge (i.e., knowledge of how things are in the actual world he brings about). The Molinist notion of a prevolitional middle knowledge was novel within Reformed circles, however. Stanglin and McCall sum it up well: "Natural knowledge includes knowledge of all that must be (in the sense of logical necessity) as well as all that could be (in the sense of logical possibility), while free knowledge is God's knowledge of what will be. Between these, however, is middle knowledge: it is God's knowledge of all that would be."[31]

Whether Arminius really did endorse middle knowledge has been the subject of some debate in recent studies of his thought.[32] However, it seems clear that Arminius did endorse the doctrine. He says things like this: "It is necessary for that middle [knowledge] to intervene in things which depend on the liberty of created choice."[33] That being said, Eef Dekker has argued that the internal logic of Arminius's position with respect to divine ordination and human freedom is actually disordered and collapses into a species of metaphysical determinism. Though Arminius would have denied this, Dekker concludes that the internal tensions in Arminius's theology drive him in this direction. While he "suggests a kind of epistemological indeterminism on the human side" this does not "loosen the ties of metaphysical determinism" all things considered, and may "lead to further incoherencies" in his thought.[34]

Be that as it may, we can summarize some of the central claims about the doctrine of creation in Arminius's theology in the following numbered statements:

1. God is a simple pure act.
2. God is free and exists *a se*.
3. God perfectly delights in God's own perfection.
4. God's perfect self-delight does not require the creation of a world in which to display this self-delight.
5. Hence, creation is a free act:
    a. God could refrain from creating a world; and
    b. God could refrain from creating this world.
6. God creates according to God's good pleasure and will, reflecting God's own character (this is God's intellectualism).
7. God creates the world *per se* good; evil is generated *per accidens*.
8. Creation and conservation are two distinct, temporal divine actions.

9. God eternally and prevolitionally knows all that is necessary and possible.
10. God eternally and prevolitionally knows all that would obtain in all logically possible states of affairs were God to bring them about.
11. God eternally and postvolitionally knows what will obtain in the world God creates.
12. God creates the world ex nihilo.

Apart from the innovative use of middle knowledge (expressed in 9–11 above) and his departure from the scholastic account of continuous creation (in 8), the main contours of Arminius's doctrine of creation appear to be well within the bounds of classical orthodoxy.

EDWARDS ON GOD AND CREATION

We come now to Jonathan Edwards. He also defended a classical account of the divine nature and attributes, including in both his unpublished and published works the claim that God is an atemporal, simple pure act.[35] Thus, in his *Miscellanies* notebook, entry 94, Edwards says, the "Holy Spirit is the act of God between the Father and the Son infinitely loving and delighting in each other." What is more, the Holy Spirit is "distinct from each of the other two [divine persons], and yet it is God; for the pure and perfect act of God is God, because God is a pure act. It appears that this is God, because that which acts perfectly is all act, and nothing but act."[36]

What is more, like Arminius, he thought of divine simplicity as primarily a piece of apophatic theology, emphasizing that the divine nature is noncomposite.[37] Edwards endorses divine aseity, but he understands this unambiguously in terms of his doctrine of theological determinism, so that divine freedom amounts to God necessarily acting according to the perfection of his nature.[38] As is well known, Edwards argues in his dissertation, *Concerning the End for Which God Created the World*, that God's ultimate end in creation is God's own self-glorification.[39] What is less well known is that Edwards is also committed to the following controversial theological claims in his doctrine of creation: that (a) God is essentially creative so that God must create some world;[40] and that (b) any theater of divine creation must be one in which the full panoply of divine attributes are displayed including God's justice and wrath as well as God's grace and mercy.

Let us consider these claims in turn. Edwards thinks that God is essentially creative. By this he means that God's nature is such that God must "self-communicate" in some act of creation. It is not merely that a creative God might generate some world or other, though God could refrain from doing so. Rather, God must create a world. In this way, Edwards's God is like an artist for whom creative action is not merely appropriate or expected, but inevitable given the sort of talents and character God has. Some artists speak of their work as being something compulsive. It is as if they cannot help themselves; in some sense they feel compelled to make works of art. Edwards seems to have something similar in mind regarding the Deity. God must create; it is God's character to create; God cannot but create, though not through compulsion. God creates because God is essentially self-diffusive. However, this would appear to infringe on two fundamental concerns of much classical Christian theology, namely, divine freedom and the claim that God exists *a se*. If God is free then (so it is often thought) God must be able to create and refrain from creating. If the act of creation is pictured as something akin to a compulsive act, then something has gone awry with our reasoning. For, so this story goes, a God who is perfect must be perfectly free to create or not as God sees fit. It is often thought that a corollary to divine freedom is divine aseity. God is free because God is independent of anything that is created. God does not depend upon creation for happiness and fulfillment, and to deny this is to deny something basic to the divine nature.

Does Edwards's theology end up denying one or both of these constituents of the tradition? On the face of it, it looks like it does. Nevertheless, in this case, first appearances may be deceptive. To begin with, Edwards maintains that divine freedom is consistent with determinism. That is, God acts in a way commensurate with necessity but without this infringing divine freedom. He says, "'Tis no disadvantage or dishonor to a being, necessarily to act in the most excellent and happy manner, from the necessary perfection of his own nature."[41] He also makes use of a distinction between natural and moral ability and inability to do a thing. God may be naturally able to do certain things, like lie or act wickedly. However, God is morally incapable of such acts given God's necessarily benevolent nature. Far from making divine actions inevitable and therefore without moral significance, Edwards thinks that the closer the morality of an action is to necessity, the more praiseworthy it is. "Men don't think a good act to be the less praiseworthy, for the agent's being much determined in it by a good inclination or a good motive" he says, "but the more."[42]

For Edwards, what matters in considering questions of freedom and moral responsibility, whether human or divine, is that the agent in question would have been able to perform the action in question if she or he had willed to do so. This is true, Edwards thinks, irrespective of whether the agent in question could have performed that action. That is, God could have created a world of unrelieved wickedness if God had willed to do so. However, God's nature is such that God is incapable of bringing this about. It is morally impossible for God to act in this way, though there is no natural impediment to God's doing so.[43]

What, then, of divine aseity? Edwards is clear that God has no need of creation in the sense that without the creation God would be unhappy or unfulfilled: "God stands in no need of his creatures, and is not profited by them; neither can his happiness be said to be added to by the creature."[44] Yet, God must create a world, given the sort of nature God has, which is essentially creative. Nevertheless, God does not depend upon the creation in and of itself for happiness or glory. It is the means by which God communicates that glory and unites with that which God has created. God does not need this world any more than artists needs paintings in order to continue to exist, though they may be said to be an expression of their character. Thus, in *Concerning the End for Which God Created the World*, Edwards remarks,

> There is something in that disposition in God to communicate goodness which shows him to be independent and self-moved in it, in a manner that is peculiar, and above what is in the beneficence of creatures.... God being all and alone is absolutely self-moved. The exercises of his communicative disposition are absolutely from within himself, not finding anything, or any object to excite them or draw them forth.[45]

Rather, "all that is good and worthy in the object, and the very being of the object" proceeds "from the overflowing of his goodness."[46]

It seems that, for Edwards, creation is the communication of

God's goodness outside of the divine self. What is more, any such creative act must include some space for the display of the divine attributes since, as Edwards makes plain in the closing sections of the second chapter of *Concerning the End for Which God Created the World*, God does all things for God's own glory, and this is the ultimate end of all God's works. Edwards remarks, "For it appears that all that is ever spoken of in the Scripture as an ultimate end of God's works is included in that one phrase, 'the glory of God'; which is the name by which the last end of God's works is most commonly called in Scripture: and seems to be the name which most aptly signifies the thing."[47] Even the very many apparently different ways in which God acts in creation, displaying one attribute here, another there, realizing this particular goal here, and another there, are all in fact merely parts of or subordinate ends toward this larger overarching ultimate end that God envisaged in creating the world, namely, the display *ad extra* of God's internal glory via its communication to the creatures.[48]

One of the startling implications of this deliverance of Edwardsian theology is that he thinks God creates the world so that he may be united with elected creatures in *theosis*. Although Edwards does not use the term *theosis* or *divinization*, this is clearly the upshot of his position. At the close of *Concerning the End for Which God Created the World*, he states this:

> We may judge of the end that the Creator aimed at, in the being, nature and tendency he gives the creature, by the mark or term which they constantly aim at in their tendency and eternal progress; though the time will never come when it can be said it is attained to, in the most absolutely perfect manner.[49]

He goes on to say,

> But if strictness of union to God be viewed as thus infinitely exalted; then the creature must be regarded as infinitely, nearly and closely united to God. And viewed thus, their interest must be viewed as one with God's interest; and so is not regarded properly with a disjunct and separate, but an undivided respect.[50]

This is a significant theological claim for someone formed in the tradition of Reformed scholasticism.

An account of Edwards's doctrine of creation would be incomplete without some mention of his twin doctrines of continuous creation and occasionalism.[51] Unlike Arminius, Edwards thinks continuous creation is one, eternal divine act. In contrast with the scholastic doctrine, Edwards construes this in terms of a continuous creation out of nothing, denying conservation. He adds to this the claim that God is the only real cause of what comes to pass (i.e., occasionalism), pressing his doctrine of creation in the direction of a four-dimensionalist account of the persistence of created things across time. That is, unlike Arminius, Edwards thinks the world does not exist whole and complete at each moment of time that it does exist. Rather, he thinks talk of "the world" is shorthand for a series of momentary world stages that exist across a period of time and that are segued together according to divine convention. This is brought out particularly clearly in his treatise on *Original Sin*:

> If the existence of created substance, in each successive moment, be wholly the effect of God's immediate power, in that moment, without any dependence on prior existence, as much as the first creation out of nothing, then what exists at this moment, by his power, is a *new effect*; and simply and absolutely considered, not the same with any past existence, though it be like it, and follows it according to a certain established method. And there is no identity or oneness in the case, but what depends on the *arbitrary* constitution of the Creator; who by his wise sovereign establishment so unites these successive new effects, that he *treats them as one*, by communicating to them like properties, relations and circumstances; and so leads us to regard and treat them as one.[52]

Later in the same passage, he underlines the following point: "Thus it appears, if we consider matters strictly, that there is no such thing as any identity or oneness in created objects, existing at different times, but what depends on God's sovereign constitution...for it appears, that a divine constitution is what makes truth, in affairs of this nature."[53]

Nothing persists through time—not the constituents of the world, not even the world itself. It would appear that, according to Edwards's way of thinking, "the world" is strictly speaking a sort of approximation. Rather than describing an entity that persists through time, from creation to conflagration, "the world" is actually shorthand for a series of momentary, but complete, worlds that God segues together making it appear that there is action across time, though, strictly speaking "divine constitution is what makes truth" in this matter.

An analogy will help to make this point clearer. Imagine a nineteenth century kinetoscope. This was an early motion picture device mounted in a wooden box with a hole through which a viewer could see a "moving picture." It was, in fact, a primitive version of the sorts of images seen on a regular basis on the silver screen of movie theaters. The pictures were photographic stills of action across time that, when run together, produced the illusion of movement and action. Edwards's understanding of continuous creation implies something like this about the world in which we live. It is a series of such "stills" that are numerically distinct, woven together, as it were, by divine convention.

There are at least two ways one could understand this. On the one hand, one might argue that this view of divine continuous creation makes of the world a sort of divine plaything that undermines real creaturely action across time. Any person at one moment is strictly speaking numerically distinct from what we would perceive to be the same person at the next moment, according to the Edwardsian way of thinking. This might be thought to be a cost to the Edwardsian if it implies that nothing persists through time, making everything radically dependent on the will of God. By contrast, one might simply accept the sort of metaphysical picture of the world that Edwards presupposes, allowing that some sort of four-dimensionalism is true. Perhaps, we might consider, things persist through time not by being numerically the same at each moment at which they exist but by having parts in time as they have physical parts at a given time. Just as I have a right arm and a left arm, both of which are different physical parts of me, I also have a part of me that existed yesterday and a part that exists today. These are what are often called temporal parts of me. Then, to speak of "me" is to speak of some four-dimensional object that extends across time as well as across space. It is a thing that has physical parts at a given time and temporal parts across a particular stretch of time. This, or something very like it, is the sort of view Edwards appears to endorse.[54] It is somewhat counterintuitive. But its appeal or lack thereof depends in large measure on whether one is willing to accept the sort of four-dimensionalist view of the world to which Edwards subscribes.

Edwards also embraces a doctrine of panentheism. This is the claim that the world is somehow an emanation from God. In his dissertation, *Concerning the End for Which God Created the World* (and elsewhere[55]), Edwards makes it clear that he thinks the world is something like an emanation from God, a shadow-like entity that is the necessary product of divine creativity:

> The emanation or communication of the divine fullness, consisting in the knowledge of God, love to God, and joy in God, has relation indeed both to God and the creature: but it has relation to God as its fountain, as it is an emanation from God; and as the communication itself, or thing communicated, is something divine, something of God, something of his internal fullness; as the water in the stream is something of the fountain; and as the beams are of the sun.... Here is both an emanation and remanation. The refulgence shines upon and into the creature, and is reflected back to the luminary. The beams of glory come from God, and are something of God, and are refunded back again to their original. So that the whole is of God, and in God, and to God; and God is the beginning, middle and end in this affair.[56]

Even if Edwards's panentheism does not push him beyond orthodoxy, it should be clear from this sketch of his doctrine of creation that it looks very different from the sort of view one would expect from a representative of Reformed orthodoxy. In many ways it is closer to the sort of position one finds elaborated by Baruch Spinoza in his *Ethics* than that of Edwards's compatriots in Puritan and continental Reformed theology. As John Cooper says in summing up Edwards's position, "All things considered, his affirmation that 'the whole is of God, and in God, and to God' is best construed philosophically as a panentheism that borders on Spinozan pantheism."[57]

We can sum up what we have seen of Edwards's views as follows:

1. God is a timeless, simple pure act.
2. God is free and exists *a se* (where divine freedom is understood to be consistent with determinism).
3. God is essentially creative so that God must create some world in order to "communicate" the divine self *ad extra*.
4. Any theater of divine creation must be one in which the full panoply of divine attributes are displayed, including God's justice and wrath as well as God's grace and mercy.

5. God creates for the ultimate end of displaying God's glory.
6. God communicates the divine self to elect creatures that he may be united to them via *theosis*.
7. Nothing persists through time.
8. The present world is a momentary stage in a series of such stages created seriatim ex nihilo by God and segued together according to divine convention.
9. God is the only causal agent in the world.
10. The world is the emanation of God's essential creativity. It is a shadowy projection from God *ad extra*.

Although there is significant conceptual overlap with Arminius (because both theologians share a common heritage and commitment to the broad contours of a classical doctrine of God), it is clear that Edwards's understanding of God and creation is innovative in several important respects—indeed, much more innovative than the doctrine espoused by Arminius.

CONCLUSION

This comparison is limited in scope and for that reason alone drawing conclusions from it is a somewhat hazardous endeavor. A complete account of Arminius's doctrine of creation, or that of Edwards, would require much more attention to detail, to aspects of their respective positions that we have only sketched, and to the important ways in which other fundamental motifs in their theologies play a part in what they say about the doctrine of creation; for example, the Trinity. However, what even this brief survey shows is that the claim that Arminius was a theological maverick or a thinker who played fast-and-loose with the tradition he inherited cannot be sustained when it comes to this doctrine, which is of fundamental importance for his theological system. The most important innovation he makes in his account of creation is the inclusion of a doctrine of middle knowledge. This does take him beyond the Reformed mainstream, and those contemporary evangelical theologians who claim to be both Molinist and Reformed would do well to pay more attention to the historical dimension to this debate.[58] However, the more startling conclusion of our comparison is that the supposed paragon of Reformed, evangelical theology, Jonathan

Edwards, has a doctrine of creation far more exotic than that of Arminius. We might put it like this: Edwards's hypertrophied account of absolute divine sovereignty expressed in his doctrines of divine determinism, the necessity of creation, and the attenuated, ephemeral nature of the creation, which is emanated by God, lead him to embrace panentheism—a doctrine often thought to be at odds with orthodox Christian theology.[59] Some critics of Edwards, like Charles Hodge, have even claimed that his work collapses into pantheism, given his idealism and robust doctrine of continuous creation.[60] Even if his view is panentheist, rather than pantheist, I submit that it requires a much more significant shift in theology than the addition of a doctrine of middle knowledge and temporal account of divine conservation to a basically classical account of the divine nature.

The comparison is instructive. Both thinkers are theologians steeped in the Reformed and western catholic theological traditions. Both are schooled in scholastic debate and utilize the technical vocabulary of Reformed orthodox discussion. Both are also biblical theologians in the sense that they are deeply engaged with the scriptural tradition, seeking to form their theological judgments in ways that reflect the shape and coherence of what they find in Scripture. Moreover, both were willing to innovate within the traditions that shaped them, where they thought that appropriate. In the doctrine of creation, it transpires that the innovations presented by Arminius were actually less radical than those allowed by Edwards.

I have argued that Arminius's doctrine of creation is an expression of a broadly orthodox account, in the post-Reformation Reformed tradition of what is sometimes referred to as Thomist Calvinism. He is able to hold together divine aseity and freedom in creation, as well as the dependence of creatures upon God. His understanding of the motivation or end of God in creation is also suitably nuanced and careful. By contrast, Edwards retains divine freedom and aseity at the cost of making creation the necessary product of divine creativity. Indeed, as a number of several studies have argued, Edwardsianism entails panentheism.[61] This is not necessarily unorthodox, but it does put Edwards's understanding of God and creation much further from the center of classical, orthodox accounts of the divine nature (including classical, orthodox Reformed accounts!) than that of Arminius. This does not show that Arminius is closer to the Reformed mainstream than Edwards, all things considered. But it does give some credence to Stanglin and McCall's view that Arminius is not the bogeyman of much Calvinist apologetic on a central doctrinal locus, namely, the doctrine of creation. Rightly or wrongly, Edwards is often regarded as a paradigm of Reformed theology, while Arminius is thought to be its antithesis. It is ironic that Edwards spent much of his intellectual capital combatting what he perceived to be "Arminianism," which was not the same as Arminius's theology, but a sort of freethinking theological sensibility that implied an anthropological turn that Edwards (rightly) regarded as a threat. This is ironic because the doctrine of creation espoused by the historical Harmenszoon is actually closer to catholic orthodoxy, including the orthodoxy of Reformed theology, than that of Jonathan Edwards.

NOTES

1. I am grateful to Jordan Wessling, Keith Stanglin, and Mark Mann for comments on a previous draft of this chapter.

2. One aspect of Arminius's legacy was the Synod of Dort and its canons. Arminius himself lived and died a Reformed pastor and professor. His immediate disciples, including the formidable Episcopius, formed the Remonstrant party that was the object of the Synod's ire. Arminius was dead and buried by that stage. His importance for the Remonstrant movement was arguably less the specifics of the doctrine he espoused than the broad theological trajectory in which his views were thought to tend.

3. A good overview of recent scholarship on Arminius can be found in Keith D. Stanglin, "Arminius and Arminianism: An Overview of Current Research," in *Arminius, Arminianism, and Europe: Jacob Arminius (1559/60–1609)*, ed. Th. Marius van Leeuwen, Keith D. Stanglin, and Marijke Tolsma, Brill's Series in Church History 39 (Leiden: Brill, 2009), 3–24.

4. Stanglin and McCall. A first draft of this paper was read at a panel discussion of this volume at the Evangelical Theological Society Annual Conference in Milwaukee, November 2012.

5. See Collin Hansen, *Young, Restless, Reformed: A Journalist's Journey with the New Calvinists* (Wheaton, Ill.: Crossway, 2008). Edwards's portrait even adorns the cover of the book.

6. See, e.g., John Piper, *God's Passion for His Glory: Living the Vision of Jonathan Edwards* (Wheaton: Crossway, 1998), which includes the complete text of Edwards's dissertation, *Concerning the End for Which God Created the World*.

7. GCP, 211.

8. *Disp. pub.*, IV.11; *Works*, 2:115. For useful discussion of this issue, cf. Stanglin and McCall, 57–59.

9. *Disp. pub.*, IV.7; *Works*, 2:114.

10. Ibid., IV.25; *Works*, 2:119.

11. Ibid., IV.28; *Works*, 2:119.

12. *Disp. priv.*, XV.9; *Works*, 2:339.

13. Ibid., XVI.3; *Works*, 2:340.

14. In this matter they follow Muller's reading of Arminius. See Stanglin and McCall, 55.

15. *Disp. pub.*, IV.11; *Works*, 2:115, emphasis added.

16. Ibid., IV.13; *Works*, 2:116.

17. See, e.g., the terse statement of this doctrine in *Disp. priv.*, XXIV.3; *Works*, 2:355; and *Certain Examples to be Diligently Examined and Weighed*, VI.1, in *Works*, 2:711. Muller has an interesting discussion of some untypical features of Arminius's conception of creation out of nothing. It appears that Arminius thought of the *nihil* from which God creates as Aristotelian primary matter. See *GCP*, 215–16.

18. *Disp. priv.*, XXIV.4; *Works*, 2:355.

19. *GCP*, 213–14.

20. *Disp. priv.*, XXIV.10; *Works*, 2:357.

21. Stanglin and McCall, 79.

22. Ibid, 80.

23. Ibid, 81.

24. *Exam. Gom.*, *Works*, 3:707.

25. In the *Dec. sent.*, in Gunter, 116, Arminius writes, "Reprobation is a hateful act that springs from hate. But the act of creation did not grow out of hatred, and it should not be construed as a way or means to accomplish the decree of reprobation. Creation is a perfect act of God that declares his wisdom, goodness, and omnipotence." All references to *Dec. sent.* in this chapter are to Gunter's edition.

26. *Disp. pub.*, IV.63; *Works*, 2:129–30; Stanglin and McCall, 71.

27. *Dec. sent.*, in Gunter, 117. Cf. Stanglin and McCall, 69–70.

28. *Disp. priv.*, XXVIII.3; *Works*, 2:367.

29. Cf. Muller who writes, "Arminius appears, consciously, to have narrowed the scope of providence specifically to temporal divine activity in and with the things of the created order and to have maintained this narrow definition by modifying the concept of *continua creatio*" (*GCP*, 248).

30. Eef Dekker drew attention to this in his paper, "Was Arminius a Molinist?," *Sixteenth Century Journal* 27, no. 2 (1996): 337–52. He writes, "Arminius not only mentions the theory of middle knowledge, but he also has incorporated it into his theology. It appears in all crucial formulations of his doctrine of divine knowledge.... Middle knowledge is vital for

Arminius since it is a cornerstone in his attempt to build a theory with the help of which he can show that both God and human beings are free" (Ibid., 351).

31. Stanglin and McCall, 67.

32. See William Gene Witt, "Creation, Redemption, and Grace in The Theology of Jacob Arminius," 2 vols. (Ph.D. diss., University of Notre Dame, 1993). Dekker's paper, "Was Arminius a Molinist?" is in part a response to Witt's claims.

33. *Disp. pub.*, IV.45, cited in Stanglin and McCall, 68.

34. Eef Dekker, "Jacob Arminius and His Logic: Analysis of a Letter," *Journal of Theological Studies* 44 (1993): 118–42, especially 138. This is disputed by Thomas H. McCall in his essay in the present volume ("Was Arminius an Unwitting Determinist?"), in which he argues that the broader consensus of Arminius's writings tell against the narrow reading of the letter Dekker focuses upon.

35. This has been disputed in several recent studies of Edwards's work, especially that of Amy Plantinga Pauw, *The Supreme Harmony of All: The Trinitarian Theology of Jonathan Edwards* (Grand Rapids: Eerdmans, 2002); and Michael J. McClymond, "Hearing the Symphony: A Critique of Some Critics of Sang Lee's and Amy Plantinga Pauw's Accounts of Jonathan Edwards View of God," in *Jonathan Edwards as Contemporary: Essays in Honor of Sang Hyun Lee*, ed. Don Schweitzer (New York: Peter Lang, 2010), 67–92. However, there is good evidence that Edwards did endorse this claim. For arguments to this conclusion, see Oliver D. Crisp, "Jonathan Edwards on Divine Simplicity," *Religious Studies* 39, no. 1 (2003): 23–41; Oliver D. Crisp, *Jonathan Edwards on God and Creation* (New York: Oxford University Press, 2012); and Kyle Strobel, *Jonathan Edwards's Theology: A Reinterpretation* (London: Bloomsbury and T&T Clark, 2013).

36. YE, 13:260. The complete *Works* are also available online at the Yale Jonathan Edwards Center website, http://edwards.yale.edu/. This is a pioneering, open-access platform that is fully searchable and includes many more of the sermons and notebooks of Edwards than the letterpress edition does.

37. For discussion of this point, see Crisp, *Jonathan Edwards on God and Creation*, ch. 5.

38. Jonathan Edwards, *Freedom of the Will*, YE, 1:377.

39. *Concerning the End for Which God Created the World* can be found in YE, vol. 8.

40. In fact, Edwards goes beyond this to claim God must create this world because it is the best possible world. Interested readers should consult William Wainwright, "Jonathan Edwards, William Rowe, and the Necessity of Creation," in *Faith, Freedom, and Responsibility*, ed. Jeff Jor-

dan and Daniel Howard-Snyder (Lanham, Md.: Rowman and Littlefield, 1996). Cf. Crisp, *Jonathan Edwards on God and Creation*, chs. 3–4.

41. YE, 1:377.

42. YE, 1:361.

43. See William Rowe's helpful discussion of Edwards on this point in *Can God Be Free?* (Oxford: Oxford University Press, 2004), 50, and Richard Muller's paper, "Jonathan Edwards and the Absence of Free Choice: A Parting of Ways in the Reformed Tradition," *Jonathan Edwards Studies* 1, no. 1 (2011): 3–22.

44. *Miscellany* 679, in YE, 18:237–38.

45. *Concerning the End for Which God Created the World*, in YE, 8:462.

46. Ibid.

47. Ibid., 8:526.

48. See ibid., 8:527–28. For a recent discussion of this theme see William M. Schweitzer, *God is a Communicative Being: Divine Communicativeness and Harmony in the Theology of Jonathan Edwards* (London: T&T Clark, 2012).

49. *Concerning the End for Which God Created the World*, in YE, 8:535. For discussion of the Edwardsian doctrine of *theosis*, see Crisp, *Jonathan Edwards on God and Creation*, ch. 8; and Kyle Strobel "Jonathan Edwards and the Polemics of *Theosis*," *Harvard Theological Review* 105, no. 3 (2012): 259–79.

50. *Concerning the End for Which God Created the World*, in YE, 8:535.

51. I have attempted a more comprehensive account in Crisp, *Jonathan Edwards on God and Creation*.

52. YE, 3:402–403, italics original.

53. Jonathan Edwards, *Original Sin*, in YE, 3:404, italics original. I have discussed these passages in *Original Sin* at greater length in Crisp, *Jonathan Edwards and the Metaphysics of Sin* (Aldershot: Ashgate, 2005).

54. In *Jonathan Edwards and the Metaphysics of Creation* (Aldershot: Ashgate, 2005), I argue for these claims more expansively. However, Michael C. Rea has argued that Edwardsian four-dimensionalism is closer to a stage theory than a temporal parts theory. This involves the same metaphysical picture of the world, carved up rather differently into momentary stages rather than temporal parts of a four-dimensional whole. See his "The Metaphysics of Original Sin," in *Persons: Human and Divine*, ed. Peter van Inwagen and Dean Zimmerman (Oxford: Oxford University Press, 2007), ch. 14. Rea refers to the fact that such four-dimensionalism can be found in other eighteenth century thinkers; e.g., David Hume.

55. Some of what he says might suggest pantheism rather than panentheism, but the preponderance of what he says on this matter is toward the latter, not the former. See, e.g., YE, 8:421 and 439; *Miscellany* 27a, in YE, 13:213; *Miscellany* 697, in YE, 18:281; and *Miscellany* 880, in YE, 20:123.

56. *Concerning the End for Which God Created the World*, in YE, 8:531.

57. John W. Cooper, *Panentheism: The Other God of the Philosophers, From Plato to the Present* (Grand Rapids: Baker Academic, 2009), 77.

58. See, e.g., Terrance L. Tiessen, *Providence and Prayer: How Does God Work in The World?* (Downers Grove, Ill.: IVP, 2000).

59. One standard definition of panentheism states that the "being of God includes and penetrates the whole universe, so that every part exists in Him, but His Being is more than, and not exhausted by, the universe" (F. L. Cross and E. A. Livingstone, eds., *The Oxford Dictionary of the Christian Church, Third Edition* [New York: Oxford University Press, 1997], 1213). This is the position Edwards advocates in *Concerning the End for Which God Created the World*.

60. See Charles Hodge, *Systematic Theology*, vol. 2 (Grand Rapids: Eerdmans, 1940 [1871]), 220. For a recent discussion of other objections to Edwardsian metaphysics as pantheistic, see Steven Studebaker and Robert Caldwell III, *The Trinitarian Theology of Jonathan Edwards: Texts, Context, and Application* (Farnham, UK: Ashgate, 2012), ch. 9.

61. In addition to Crisp, *Jonathan Edwards on God and Creation*, see, e.g., John J. Bombaro, *Jonathan Edwards's Vision of Reality: The Relationship of God to the World, Redemption History, and the Reprobate*, Princeton Theological Monographs Series (Eugene, Oreg.: Pickwick Publications, 2012); Cooper, *Panentheism*, 74–77; and Douglas Elwood, *The Philosophical Theology of Jonathan Edwards* (New York: University of Columbia Press, 1960).

CHAPTER 6

CONVERGENCE IN THE "REFORMED" THEOLOGIES OF T. F. TORRANCE AND JACOB ARMINIUS

E. Jerome Van Kuiken

One of the motives behind this volume is to seek common ground between those who self-identify as Reformed and those who see themselves as heirs of Arminius.[1] A great barrier to achieving this purpose is the Reformed rejection at the Synod of Dort (1618–1619) of views associated with Arminius. I propose to step both beyond and behind Dort in order to build a bridge over that barrier by noting convergence between a representative of Neo-Reformed theology, T. F. Torrance, and Arminius on the topics of predestination, the scope of the atonement, and the interrelation of divine and creaturely agency (corresponding to the U, L, and I in the post-Dort mnemonic TULIP). So as not to disrupt the integrity of each theologian's system, I shall describe each of them in turn before comparing them and drawing conclusions.

In this chapter's title, the term *Reformed* is being used in a qualified sense in relation to our two theologians. It bears repeating that Torrance represents *Neo*-Reformed theology, *not* traditional

113

Reformed theology. On Arminius's part, the appellation of "Reformed" to his theology is of course controversial. Keith Stanglin, after surveying the debate between Carl Bangs and Richard Muller on this point, has nevertheless suggested that a degree of consensus exists: Arminius was "Reformed" in at least the loose sense of the ecclesial and colloquial usage of that term in his lifetime.[2] At this chapter's outset, it is this loose sense that obtains; in the conclusion, we shall consider whether Arminius may be considered Reformed in a somewhat stricter, more theological sense. Meanwhile, we shall examine first Torrance's more recent theology before moving farther back in history to Arminius's views.

T. F. TORRANCE AND REFORMED THEOLOGY

Thomas F. Torrance (1913–2007) has been hailed as a leading Reformed theologian of the twentieth century.[3] Among his Reformed credentials is his lifelong membership in the Church of Scotland, which he served in various capacities, including as a minister, a theology professor at New College, Edinburgh (1952–1979), and a Moderator (1976–1977). Additionally, he represented his denomination and the World Alliance of Reformed Churches in ecumenical dialogues and edited volumes of Calvin's writings.[4] Nevertheless, Torrance was hardly "old-school" Reformed: A former student of Karl Barth's, he was a key player in mediating Barth's theology to Great Britain, not least by supervising the translation of the *Church Dogmatics* into English.[5] Torrance was also openly critical of Reformed scholasticism, particularly of its federal theology, and of its greatest legacy in Scotland: the Westminster Confession of Faith, the subordinate doctrinal standard of the Church of Scotland. Torrance faulted the Westminster Standards for what he considered to be their displacement of a christocentric theology by anthropocentric "logico-causal," legalistic thinking, especially in their predestinarian doctrine.[6] In what follows, we shall describe Torrance's criticisms of past Reformed theologizing (in which he intemperately deploys the language of heresy), as well as his constructive dogmatic proposals.

TORRANCE ON THE NATURE AND SCOPE OF ELECTION AND PREDESTINATION

Crucial for Torrance is the indivisible unity of being, act, and word in God. Jesus Christ is one in being (*homoousios*) with God the Father and so shares that indivisibility.[7] Therefore God's decreeing word of predestination, God's act of election, cannot be in any sense antecedent or unrelated to the eternal divine Word and Act who is Christ. As the *logos*, he himself is the whole and sole logic or reason behind predestination.[8] To say otherwise is either Arian (the uncoupling of what God is toward himself in his very being from what God is toward us in his revelatory, reconciling act in Christ) or else Marcionite (the bifurcation of God into "two 'Gods', one who comes to us in Christ, and some dark predestinarian 'God' who acts behind the back of Christ and his cross").[9]

Election, then, begins in eternity in the person of Jesus Christ, who is both the subject and object of election.[10] As God the Son, Christ elects in unity of action with the Father. As the Elect One, Christ is from the beginning the *logos incarnandus*, the "going-to-be-enfleshed" Word.[11] The eternal election of the humanity of Christ is by implication the eternal election of all of humanity in Christ, and indeed, of all of creation in Christ. This is so because Christ is the Word through whom all things were made and are sustained, so that Christ's union with one portion of creation affects the whole of it.[12] Inasmuch as humanity and the rest of the created order have fallen under affliction by evil, God's intention to become incarnate is also the election of *sinful* humanity and its cosmos in Christ; it is God's gracious decision to identify in merciful love with estranged creatures, taking their cause and corruption upon the divine self in order to redeem them for a filial relationship that partakes of the union of God the Son with the Father.[13]

This eternal election of and in the Son enters into time as *prothesis*, as predestination, the temporal forth-putting of the divine purpose.[14] It enters time first in the election of Israel, then narrows down to the election of a single Israelite, Jesus of Nazareth, as the vicarious human who acts as representative of and substitute for all. His incarnation manifests the principle that reprobation occurs *within election*. Throughout his earthly life, Christ the vicarious human bears sinlessly the external contradiction of sinners, the internal contradiction of sinful human nature, and the divine judgment upon sin. The cross is the culmination of this life-act of bearing sin and God's wrath upon it and of reconciling sinful humanity to God.[15] Christ's resurrection signals that the reconciliation and regeneration of the whole created order have been accomplished in Christ.[16] Thus God's election is identical with Christ and the cross:

"*Prothesis* means that not only in Christ the beloved are we eternally loved and elected, but that Christ is the *way* in which we are loved and elected. He is the way, the door, and there is no other way to the Father, no other door to salvation, than he."[17]

The gospel, then, is that in Christ all people have been unconditionally elected to communion with God. To preach the gospel is to confront individuals with the truth of their election through the costly work of Christ. This proclamation provokes a crisis in its recipients; some respond in repentant faith and come to enjoy the benefits of their election, while others inexplicably reject the truth that they are elect and opt instead to live in denial, damning themselves to the hell of reprobation that Christ already has borne fully for them. Because reprobation lies within election, their refusal does not render them nonelect, but simply cut off from the benefits of their election.[18]

In contrast with his own doctrine of predestination, Torrance critiques past formulations of the doctrine that "project back into God the kind of logical or causal connections, or even the kind of temporal connections which we have on earth, for then we make it into some kind of pre-determinism or fatalism, which is very wrong, and quite unchristian."[19] Rather than operating through metaphysical mechanics, predestination functions through personal agency: In the New Testament, Jesus and his followers entered into fellowship with sinners, thus bringing them into a personal encounter with the reality of election—a reality that demands a personal decision in the face of its claims.[20]

TORRANCE ON THE SCOPE OF THE ATONEMENT

Torrance's teaching on the scope of the atonement coheres with his belief in universal unconditional election. If through the Word all things were made, then through the incarnate Word all things are reconciled—including all humanity, for the Word sustains and has assumed the nature common to all human beings, not just some specially graced few. When the New Testament says that Christ died for all people, this claim must be taken at face value.[21]

In this light, Torrance severely criticizes the notion of a limited atonement, which he does not scruple to call a heresy. To limit the atonement is to limit the triune love that is the very being of God. It is to divide the Father from the Son, for if the Son only bears God's wrath for a portion of humanity, then there remains a judgment by the Father apart from Christ and the cross, in which case not all judgment has been granted to the Son by the Father (contrary to John 5:22). It is also to promote Nestorianism by dividing the Son's divine nature and acts from his human nature and acts. This Nestorianism takes two forms: Firstly, "hyper-Calvinist" soteriology claims that Christ suffered only in his humanity, so that his deity remained uninvolved and the human sufficiency of his sacrifice was not coextensive with its divine efficacy; secondly, the Son as human did not atone for all that the Son as divine has created and upholds.[22]

While Torrance absolutely rejects limited atonement, he also dismisses the view that the cross merely *potentially* saves all, with the actualization of that potential left up to individuals' decisions. To think in this way "is to land in Arminianism and to teach that ultimately everyone is their own saviour, in so far as they have to cooperate with Christ for their salvation. But if all that has been done in the death of Christ is the creation of the possibility of salvation, then who can be sure of their salvation, since everything depends in the last analysis on human weakness?"[23] Instead, the atonement is objectively sufficient and efficacious for everyone: All humans are united with Christ in his substitutionary, representative humanity and cannot escape that fact. Those who reject it are, in the end, damned in spite of the universal efficacy of the atonement.[24]

TORRANCE ON THE LOGIC OF GRACE

The doctrine of limited atonement is, Torrance claims, grounded in "a philosophical or metaphysical conception of irresistible grace and of absolute divine causality, such that it could not but be held that all for whom Christ died efficaciously must necessarily be saved."[25] But the opposite heresy, universalism, depends on the same erroneous reasoning. Both doctrines commit the category mistake of applying to the transcendent God the kind of "logico-causal," deterministic relations that obtain in the physical world.[26] In addition, they fail to recognize the irrational nature of evil. To attempt to explain why some persons persist in unbelief into eternity is to explain away "the mystery of iniquity." Appealing to Calvin, Torrance claims that the rejection of the gospel occurs *"per accidens* or *accidentaliter*—that is, irrationally and inexplicably."[27] One cannot even appeal to human free will by way of explanation, for fallen free will is simply self-will and so cannot decide for God, but Christ's reconciling work has converted our will in himself so that it aligns with God's will.[28]

Rather than projecting deterministic causality, irresistible force, or logical necessity onto spiritual realities, Torrance looks instead to the hypostatic union for his model of the interaction of divine and creaturely agency. There he finds at work the "essential logic...of God's grace" as captured in the christological couplet "*anhypostasia-enhypostasia.*"[29] The human nature assumed by the divine Son is anhypostatic, lacking any independent person, will, or activity. Therefore all is of grace, even in the incarnation. But the act of assumption renders that human nature enhypostatic, possessing a genuine human will and activity through its union with the person of the Son.[30] Hence "all of God" and "all of grace" does not mean "none of the human" but rather "all of the human."[31]

Torrance applies this model to the God-world relationship in general and to the God-human relationship in particular. Divine providence enables cosmic contingence—the created order's limited but real freedom, sovereignly guided by God to achieve divine ends, even when that freedom generates evil.[32] Likewise, God's grace enables rather than disables authentic human action.[33] In our fallen, depersonalized condition, we cannot of ourselves adequately repent and believe the gospel, and this inadequacy undermines our assurance of salvation. Christ, however, is the "personalising Person" who has acted on our behalf, repenting and believing for us. Christ's repentant faith is echoed in us and ours is perfected in Christ as we come to share in Christ's vicarious action through the agency of the Holy Spirit.[34] In this way United Methodist theologian Elmer Colyer sees Torrance's "logic of grace" as transcending the zero-sum models of monergism and synergism.[35] Be that as it may, Torrance's account of agency allows for an individual human will to resist into eternity God's gracious will to save that individual.

While Torrance looks back at and down on Reformed scholasticism, particularly its federalist versions, Arminius stands at its headwaters as a contributor as well as a critic. Richard Muller has demonstrated that Arminius fits comfortably within the milieu of emerging Protestant scholasticism.[36] For instance, it is Arminius who first articulated the notion of an intra-Trinitarian covenant of redemption that later became a fixture of Reformed federal theology.[37] His notoriety, however, springs from his rebukes and revisions of elements of the developing Reformed tradition. We turn our investigation now to three of these elements.

ARMINIUS ON THE NATURE AND SCOPE OF ELECTION AND PREDESTINATION

Arminius was deeply dissatisfied with contemporary Reformed accounts of unconditional double predestination, especially the version later known as supralapsarianism, which he had encountered first as Beza's student in Geneva and ended his days disputing about with his colleagues at the University of Leiden.[38] He charged these accounts with impugning God's character, diminishing Christ's significance for predestination, and unbalancing Christian assurance of salvation.[39] Arminius sought to remedy these perceived defects with his own doctrine of predestination.

According to Arminius, the foundation of religion is found in God's character, specifically in the twofold love of God. The first and superordinate love is of righteousness/justice;[40] its primary object is God, whose nature is perfectly good and just; its secondary object is righteousness/justice in the created order, and its derivative is a divine hatred of all unrighteousness/injustice. The second and subordinate love is for humankind, and its derivative is displeasure at human misery. Arminius's ranking of the two loves is crucial for his doctrine of predestination: Putting the love of righteousness/justice first ensures that God elects and reprobates not arbitrarily but based on righteousness/justice or its opposite in the recipient of God's action. Moreover, God's love of humans even as fallen and accompanying hatred of their misery explain the motive for God's redemptive plan, while God's overarching love of righteousness/justice and hatred of lawlessness preserve that plan from degenerating into a Golgotha-less "cheap grace" that leaves divine justice unsatisfied. Finally, at the pastoral level, this twofold love discourages both a spiritual presumption that excuses sin through reliance on one's unconditional election (thus ignoring God's love of righteousness/justice), as well as a spiritual despair issuing from fear of one's unconditional reprobation (thus forgetting God's love of God's creatures, including sinful ones).[41]

On the basis of God's twofold love, Arminius outlines four divine decrees of predestination.[42] God has predestined: (1) the ground and executor of salvation: Christ, the appointed mediator, who merits and administers redemption on behalf of humanity; (2) the conditions of receiving salvation in Christ or damnation apart from him: repentance and faith in the former case, impenitence and unbelief in the latter; (3) the sufficient, efficacious provision of the means necessary to repent and believe: the outward proclamation of the gospel, the inward influence of the Holy Spirit, and unusual acts of God, for instance; and (4) the specific recipients of salvation (the elect) and damnation (the reprobate): on the one hand, those whom God foreknew would believe and persevere in response to his grace, and, on the other, those whom God foreknew would not.[43]

This fourfold scheme requires careful examination. It reverses the supralapsarian order, which starts with the decree of election and reprobation for specific individuals, then provides means to effect that decree (including, among other means, creation, the fall, and the appointment of Christ to merit righteousness solely for the elect).[44] Arminius argues that his own ordering gives Christ his due place as predestination's ground, not merely its executor.[45] There is no decree fixing individuals' fates antecedent to the election of Christ as mediator and deliverer.[46] The remaining three decrees deal respectively with the divinely ordained, enabled, and recompensed response of sinners to the mediation of Christ, as called for in the dominical and apostolic preaching. In short, predestination, Arminius insists, has everything to do with the revealed gospel, not with any hidden divine will; indeed, predestination properly understood is "the sum and matter of the gospel; nay, it is the gospel itself."[47]

The basis of the fourfold decree in the twofold love of God means that predestination in all its phases is conditional. The last three decrees clearly are conditioned by repentance and faith, with the fourth decree bringing in "middle knowledge" in relation to the divine foreknowledge of future contingent creaturely choices, as God's means to ensure that these conditions are met.[48] This foreknowledge, however, also governs the first decree: The Father's prescience of the Son's obedient accomplishment of his assigned task of mediation is the condition of Christ's being rewarded as Redeemer and ruler, in accordance with the covenant made between the Father and the Son.⁴⁹ The condition of faith in Christ for salvation stems, in fact, from this conditional covenant.⁵⁰

Conceptually, the quartet of decrees includes two rounds of movement from God's universal provision for salvation to God's partitive application of salvation, as shown by the following figure:

Universal Salvific Provision	Partitive Salvific Application
Decree 1: Christ wins salvation for humanity.	Decree 2: Conversion will lead to salvation; recalcitrance will lead to damnation.
Decree 3: Means are appointed whereby humanity may receive salvation.	Decree 4: All converts are saved; all recalcitrant are damned.

In contrast with supralapsarianism, which prioritizes the partitive, the priority of the universal over the partitive within this double movement implies God's genuine desire for all humanity to be saved.⁵¹ The first decree thus prepares for the doctrine of unlimited atonement, while the third decree supports the doctrine of general prevenient grace. Each of these doctrines will be considered in turn below. The presence of the partitive decrees, however, bespeaks God's commitment to treat human beings as responsible agents rather than as inanimate objects. God initiates, but God also requires and enables a fitting response and punishes responses that abuse this enablement. Reprobation, however, is subordinate to God's antecedent salvific will, as expressed in the first and third decrees, and is a reflex action when that will is humanly rejected; the divine will to reprobate is not coequal and coeval (speaking logically, not chronologically) with the divine will to save.⁵²

ARMINIUS ON THE SCOPE OF THE ATONEMENT

As indicated above, the ordering of decrees of predestination impacts one's view of the scope of the atonement. Supralapsarianism taught that, by God's will, Christ died only for those whom God had already unconditionally elected to life, abandoning the reprobate to their sin.⁵³ For instance, Puritan theologian William Perkins distinguished between the "potential efficacy" and the "actual efficacy" of the atonement. Arminius critiques Perkins's "potential efficacy" as oxymoronic and prefers the traditional scholastic formula that Christ's death was sufficient for all, but efficacious only for believers. Perkins, Arminius complains, has converted that sufficiency into a hypothetical: *If* God had willed that Christ die for all, *then* that death would have been sufficient to cover the sins of all, while, in fact, God did not so will, and therefore Christ did not die for all.[54]

Arminius offers a battery of arguments against limited atonement. Scripture repeatedly asserts that Christ died for "all" and "the world" rather than merely for the elect. The consensus of the ancient church concurs.[55] In the incarnation, the Son assumed both human nature and the curse of sin common to all, and Christ offered up that shared nature for the breaking of that shared curse for all.[56] To restrict the atonement is to restrict and therefore falsify God's attribute of *philanthropia*—that is, God's love of humanity in general—as well as to leave God's attribute of justice partially unsatisfied (in the case of the unatoned-for reprobate) and partially satisfied in an unjust manner (since the elect are atoned for unconditionally and therefore logically, to Arminius's mind, need not even obey the gospel).[57]

Arminius denies universalism, however.[58] Christ's death was a ransom that purchased salvation for humanity by satisfying divine justice, thus eliminating it as an obstacle to divine mercy and reconciling God to sinners.[59] The *application* of the atonement in the actual justifying of particular individuals depends upon faith in the Christ who died for them.[60]

ARMINIUS ON PROVIDENCE, GRACE, AND FREE WILL

We have seen that, in Arminius's fourfold scheme of predestination, the third decree expresses God's universal saving desire by providing enablement for all people to repent and believe the gospel, while the fourth decree indicates that God foreknows that some will do so and others will not. The differential factor behind these two decrees is a robust view of human free will. Divine foreknowledge is noncausative of the human choices foreseen,[61] and divine grace, while causative (not merely persuasive), is not irresistibly so, leaving room for human refusal of the gospel.[62] Arminius does not advocate free will out of any promethean impulses, however; his concern is to maintain God's sovereignty while defending God's character against any logical entailment that God authors sin.⁶³

This twofold concern appears in the title of Arminius's public disputation on providence, *On the Righteousness and Efficacy of the Providence of God concerning Evil*.⁶⁴ Here he iterates that God *permits* (not *causes*) sin based on the gift to humanity of free will. God also hinders sin insofar as is fitting, permits incitements to sin in order to test human hearts, overrules sinners' intentions by bringing good out of evil, and punishes sinners for their wrongdoing. In this manner, Arminius later writes, human free will remains under divine superintendence. God is active in sin's commencement (through divine permissions), its continuance (through setting its limits and repurposing it toward good), and its conclusion (through punishing or pardoning it).⁶⁵

God's providence over human good is no less extensive than over human evil. Arminius claims that, even in Eden, humanity was able to know, freely will, and do genuine good only by the gift of divine grace; fallen humanity has utterly lost these abilities and only regains them through the restoration of grace. God's involvement in human goodness parallels and supersedes God's involvement in human evil: God is active in every good's commencement (through prevenient grace, which frees the human agent for the good), its continuance (through cooperative grace, which works together with the human agent to perform the good), and its conclusion (through the actual achievement of the good). This three-step sequence describes the progression of every individual good action within a person's life, as well as the *ordo salutis*—God's saving work in one's life as a whole.⁶⁶ Thus, in summoning sinners to convert, God calls externally by sending preachers of the word and internally by the Spirit's softening of sinners' hearts. Grace produces within them the repentance and faith conditional to salvation— unless that grace is resisted, which is the accidental (*per accidens*) result of divine calling and leads to increased condemnation.⁶⁷ As den Boer notes, Arminius does not assert that humans have a free choice to believe, only a free choice *not* to believe.⁶⁸

Arminius supports his belief in the nonirresistibility of grace from Scripture and from the nature of grace, which does not forcibly override free will but redirects and restores it from its depraved state so that it can will the good.⁶⁹ He repudiates Pelagianism by name and writes, "That teacher obtains my highest approbation who ascribes as much as possible to Divine Grace, provided he so pleads the cause of Grace, as not to inflict an injury on the Justice of God, and not to take away *the free will to that which is evil*."[70] Clearly, what Arminius seeks via the doctrine of free will is not praiseworthiness for one's goodness and salvation but blameworthiness for one's wickedness and damnation.

TORRANCE AND ARMINIUS: AN ASSESSMENT OF THE CONVERGENCE

Having surveyed each of our theologians' views, we now may assess the degree of convergence between them. On predestination, Torrance and Arminius agree in opposing any system that demotes Christ from his rightful place as the foundation as well as the executor of humankind's predestination. Both reject a view of reprobation as unconditional and as symmetrical with, rather than subordinate to, God's universal salvific will. Both insist that predestination, properly understood, is equivalent to the gospel, not to an unknown divine will behind Christ's back and different from the evangelical revelation. Both express a pastoral concern for Christian assurance and can counsel against despair by recounting the saving love of God for all. At first glance, the unconditionality of Torrance's system would seem less equipped than the conditionality of Arminius's in effectively addressing the opposite of despair, presumption. Yet that is not the case. Although the two men's theological accents differ, the outcome is the same. Arminius urges God's primary love of righteousness/justice and, consequently, the possibility of divine judgment, to motivate the presumptuous to seek God. Torrance recognizes the possibility of self-damnation but focuses on God's substitutionary love for sinners (even the presumptuous) in order to motivate them to look in faith to Christ, not themselves.[71] Thus, both concur that presumption may result in eternal exclusion from communion with God and that the cure is reorientation toward God.

Regarding the atonement, Torrance and Arminius agree in denying any restriction to its range, with appeal to Scripture and to the commonality of the human nature taken up in the incarnation and offered up on the cross. Torrance complains of a self-salvation implicit within Arminianism's reduction of atonement to a potential awaiting actualization through one's individual decision. As with Christian assurance, though, the theoretical difference between Torrance's unconditionality and Arminius's conditionality on this point can obscure their similarities. Arminius sees Christ's atonement not as a matter of pure potentiality but as actually achieving the reconciliation of God. That achievement, and the consequent release of salvation-enabling grace into the world, are unconditioned by individual decisions in response to them. On Torrance's part, however much he may qualify it, persons' avoidance of hell paradoxically is conditional on their decision to believe in the unconditionality of the atonement. Neither theologian, though, is willing to speak of such decisions as somehow taking place apart from the intervention of grace.

Regarding grace, both Torrance and Arminius acknowledge a divinely enabled creaturely freedom within God's providence. Both confess that free will in fallen humanity is self-will and unable to choose God, so that grace is necessary in order to counteract depravity and produce repentant faith but that grace does not operate as a deterministic force. Hence Arminius could say "amen" to Torrance's claim that "all of grace" means not "none of the human" but "all of the human." We thus may speak of both men as advocating a "monergistic synergism" in which God does all that pertains to salvation, but God does it with, not without, human agency. Finally, both Torrance and Arminius grieve the reality of resistance to grace resulting *per accidens* from its activity, and both reject universalism.

What is the significance of this convergence between Torrance and Arminius? We must not overstate the implications by portraying Torrance as a crypto-Arminian or Arminius as a proto-Barthian.[72] Mention has been made of Torrance's unconditionality of election and salvation versus Arminius's conditionality in these doctrines, but I believe that this distinction is symptomatic of more basic differences between the two theologies. Torrance dreads dualisms[73] and thinks in unities, such as oneness of divine being and act, single predestination, the radical objectivity of salvation, and mono-covenantalism,[74] while Arminius, trained as a logician, thinks disjunctively: the twofold love of God, four decrees of predestination, objective provision vis-à-vis subjective appropriation of salvation, and multiple covenants. Additionally, Arminius prioritizes principles (justice, freedom, causation), while Torrance prizes personhood and spurns "logico-causal" theologizing. For instance, Arminius describes God's primary love as a love of *righteousness/justice*, a principle attributed to persons; strictly speaking, what is loved is not the person *per se* but the person's quality of righteousness/justice. By contrast, Torrance sees God's primary love as a love of *the Son*.[75] Likewise, Arminius's denial of irresistible grace springs not from a concern for the dynamics of interpersonal relationships but for upholding divine justice and, as a means to that end, human liberty.[76] Perhaps a measure of synthesis between Torrance's and Arminius's systems is possible—after all, both unity and distinction exist in the ultimate reality of the Trinity, and Torrance's personalism could ground Arminius's principalism—but that would be the stuff of a constructive project, not of the present survey of the two theologians' points of convergence.[77] In the end, despite their agreements, Torrance likely would have regarded Arminius as a heretic—ironically, not for violating the standards of (post-Dort) Reformed orthodoxy but for being too much like it in applying categories of conditionality and causality to divine action.

Torrance's free usage of the language of heresy against the positions of others (including those within the Reformed camp) requires the mention of another point at which the significance of his convergence with Arminius does not lie. Their areas of agreement over against Reformed tradition do not constitute an infallible dogmatic orthodoxy by which all dissenters must be adjudged damnably deviant. Here Torrance would have done well to learn from church history concerning how often the charge of heresy has led to slander, caricature, political machinations, and outright violence—not least in the cases of Arminius and the subsequent struggles between Dutch Remonstrants and Contra-Remonstrants.[78] Where historical and theological particulars are properly respected, it becomes clear that Arminius was as far from Pelagianism or semi-Pelagianism as were the high Calvinists from Marcionism or Nestorianism, nor was either party implicitly Arian.[79] A preferable perspective is to view Torrance's and Arminius's convergence as occurring within the matrix of orthodox convictions already shared by traditional Reformed, Neo-Reformed, and Arminius (and many of his heirs).[80]

We have indicated what the significance of our two theologians' convergence is not; what then is it? First, and least in importance, it raises the issue of whether Arminius may be Reformed in a stricter sense than granted at the beginning of our inquiry. In his important study, Richard Muller rejects Arminius's Reformed theological credentials because the Dutchman's doctrines of the God-world relationship and a universal divine salvific will are discontinuous with the development of Reformed theology from the Reformers themselves up through Arminius's day.[81] Yet Torrance, who is generally acknowledged as a Reformed theologian, converges with Arminius to a striking degree on these very points. I do not presume to dictate to the Reformed world what its boundaries should be; that is a matter to be settled internally. I only raise questions: To what extent does the word *Reformed* in the term *Neo-Reformed theology* indicate a genuine expression of the Reformed tradition? What are the limits of that tradition's openness to revision, as captured in the classic Reformed slogan *semper reformanda*—that is, "always reforming"? If there is room at the Reformed table for Torrance, may there be a stool at its foot for one whose theology converges with the Scot's at significant points? Or does Arminius's combination of scholastic means and Torrancesque ends render him forever anathema to both parties of the Reformed?

Secondly, and of far greater moment, the convergence between Torrance and Arminius has practical significance for those who derive their theologies from these two teachers. On the ecumenical front, we may hope that the clearing of a broader swath of common ground will yield increased cooperation between the two sides in the cause of Christ's kingdom. In our catechesis and apologetics, together we may teach that the tragedy of any soul's final loss must be attributed to the irrational, antichrist mystery of iniquity, not to a suprarational, ante-Christ mystery of divine will. And at the ministry of the Word and Table, with one voice we may proclaim to everyone unreservedly, "God sent the Son for *you*; Christ's body and blood were given for *you*; in the power of his Spirit, believe the good news!"

NOTES

1. For their comments on earlier versions of this material, thanks to Tom McCall, Jon Morgan, Kenny Johnston, Dick Eugenio, Bruce McCormack, and Stephen Gunter.

2. Keith D. Stanglin, "Arminius and Arminianism: An Overview of Current Research," in *Arminius, Arminianism, and Europe: Jacob Arminius (1559/60–1609)*, ed. Th. Marius van Leeuwen, Keith Stanglin, and Marijke Tolsma, Brill's Series in Church History 39 (Boston: Brill, 2009), 10–13.

3. Alister E. McGrath, *T. F. Torrance: An Intellectual Biography* (Edinburgh: T&T Clark, 1999), xi; Elmer M. Colyer, *How to Read T. F. Torrance: Understanding His Trinitarian & Scientific Theology* (Downers Grove, Ill.: InterVarsity, 2001), 11, 15, 20n14; Thomas F. Torrance, *Incarnation: The Person and Life of Christ*, ed. Robert T. Walker (Downers Grove, Ill.: InterVarsity, 2008). George Hunsinger has called him "arguably the greatest Reformed theologian since Karl Barth," in "Thomas F. Torrance: A Eulogy," *Participatio: Journal of the Thomas F. Torrance Theological Fellowship* 1 (2009): 11. Cf., on pp. 6–10 of the same volume, Alasdair Heron's eulogy.

4. Colyer, *How to Read T. F. Torrance*, 43–47. For a book-length biography of Torrance, see McGrath, *T. F. Torrance*.

5. McGrath, *T. F. Torrance*, ch. 6 (113–45, esp. 126–28); Colyer, *How to Read T. F. Torrance*, 38–40, 44–45; D. Densil Morgan, *Barth Reception in Britain* (London: T&T Clark, 2010), 1–3, 49, 183–84, 193, 220–28, 242–60. Torrance published two books on Barth: *Karl Barth: An Introduction to His Early Theology 1910-1931*, new ed. (Edinburgh: T&T Clark, 2000); and *Karl Barth, Biblical and Evangelical Theologian* (Edinburgh: T&T Clark, 1990).

6. David Fergusson, "Torrance as a Scottish Theologian," *Participatio* 2 (2010): 79–82; *The School of Faith: The Catechisms of the Reformed Church*, trans. and ed. with an introduction by Thomas F. Torrance (New York: Harper & Bros., 1959), xvi–xix, xlii, lxiii–lxiv; Thomas F. Torrance, *Scottish Theology: From John Knox to John McLeod Campbell* (Edinburgh: T&T Clark, 1996), x–xi (quotation from lattermost page).

7. Thomas F. Torrance, "The Atonement. The Singularity of Christ and the Finality of the Cross: The Atonement and the Moral Order," in *Universalism and the Doctrine of Hell*, ed. Nigel M. de S. Cameron (Grand Rapids: Baker, 1992), 231–33; Thomas F. Torrance, *Preaching Christ Today: The Gospel and Scientific Thinking* (Grand Rapids: Eerdmans, 1994), 14–19, 27, 28; Thomas F. Torrance, *The Christian Doctrine of God: One Being Three Persons* (Edinburgh: T&T Clark, 1996), 40. Cf. Thomas F. Torrance, *Atonement: The Person and Work of Christ*, ed. Robert T. Walker (Downers Grove, Ill.: InterVaristy, 2009), 211, 222, 223.

8. Torrance, *Incarnation*, 178.

9. Thomas F. Torrance, *The Trinitarian Faith: The Evangelical Theology of the Ancient Catholic Church* (Edinburgh: T&T Clark, 1988), ch. 4; Torrance, *Preaching Christ Today*, 18–21, 52–56; Torrance, *Incarnation*, 258 (quoted above); cf. Torrance, *The Christian Doctrine of God*, 4, 5, 13, 240–44.

10. Torrance, *Incarnation*, 113; Torrance, *The Christian Doctrine of God*, 144–46.

11. Torrance, *Incarnation*, 177; cf. Torrance, *The Christian Doctrine of God*, 4–6, 109n80. Torrance uses the concept, but not the Greco-Latin term, which I owe to Bruce L. McCormack. See "Grace and Being: The Role of God's Gracious Election in Karl Barth's Theological Ontology," in Bruce

L. McCormack, *Orthodox and Modern: Studies in the Theology of Karl Barth* (Grand Rapids: Baker Academic, 2008), 184–86.

12. Torrance, *Atonement*, 183; Torrance, "Singularity," 230–31, 244–45; Torrance, *Preaching Christ Today*, 14, 68–71.

13. Thomas F. Torrance, *The Mediation of Christ*, rev. ed. (Colorado Springs: Hermers & Howard, 1992), ch. 3 (47–72); Torrance, *Preaching Christ Today*, 58–59; Thomas F. Torrance, *Divine and Contingent Order* (Oxford: Oxford University Press, 1981), 134–42.

14. Torrance, *Incarnation*, 169, 171, 174, 178.

15. Ibid., 41–56, 109; Torrance, *Mediation*, 10–12, 27–42.

16. Torrance, *Atonement*, 235, 239, 286; Torrance, *Mediation*, 85.

17. Torrance, *Incarnation*, 179; cf. Torrance, *The Christian Doctrine of God*, 2.

18. Torrance, *Incarnation*, 179, 180, 110, 114; Torrance, *Mediation*, 92–95; Torrance, *Preaching Christ Today*, 35–38.

19. Torrance, *Incarnation*, 258; cf. Torrance, *Christian Doctrine*, 210.

20. Torrance, *Incarnation*, 179, 180.

21. Torrance, *Atonement*, 183; Torrance, "Singularity," 226, 244, 245, 249.

22. Torrance, *Atonement*, 185–87; Torrance, "Singularity," 244–46; cf. Torrance, *The Christian Doctrine of God*, 246–54 (in which Torrance claims patristic support for seeing God as both impassible and passible); Torrance, *Scottish Theology*, 19. Torrance's use of the label *hyper-Calvinist* differs from its technical usage, according to Donald Macleod, "Dr. T. F. Torrance and Scottish Theology: A Review Article," *Evangelical Quarterly* 72, no. 1 (2000): 57, 58.

23. Torrance, *Atonement*, 187.

24. Ibid., 188–90; cf. Torrance, *Scottish Theology*, 275; James J. Cassidy, "T. F. Torrance's Realistic Soteriological Objectivism and the Elimination of Dualisms: Union with Christ in Current Perspective," *Mid-America Journal of Theology* 19 (2008): 165–94. It should be said that Cassidy's charges of monism and monophysitism misconstrue Torrance.

25. Torrance, *Atonement*, 186.

26. Torrance claims that deterministic connections do not even exist uniformly within physical reality, e.g., in quantum physics ("Singularity," 227). This is a disputed claim: cf. Carl Hoefer, "Causal Determinism," 4.4, in *The Stanford Encyclopedia of Philosophy (Spring 2010 Edition)*, ed. Edward N. Zalta, last modified January 21, 2010, http://plato.stanford.edu/archives/spr2010/entries/determinism-causal/. In response to Torrance, Macleod denies that the Westminster Confession teaches determinism or single causality, and he, too, seeks a parallel in the alleged indeterminism of quantum physics ("Dr. T. F. Torrance and Scottish Theology," 59).

27. Torrance, "Singularity," 246–48 (quotation from lattermost page);

Torrance, *The Christian Doctrine of God*, 246. Cf. Torrance, *Mediation*, xiii–xiv; Torrance, *Incarnation*, 114; Torrance, *Scottish Theology*, 275. Torrance's appeal to Calvin blurs Calvin's claim that gospel rejection happens "by accident" with Torrance's own view that gospel rejection is irrational and inexplicable rather than suprarational and explicable in terms of God's hidden will. Cf. Alasdair Heron, "Calvin in the Theology of Thomas F. Torrance: Calvin's Doctrine of Man (1949)," *Participatio* 2 (2010): 44–63.

28. Torrance, *Mediation*, 85; Torrance, *Preaching Christ Today*, 36, 37; cf. Torrance, *Incarnation*, 253.

29. Torrance, *Karl Barth, Biblical and Evangelical Theologian*, 199.

30. Ibid.

31. Torrance, "Singularity," 230 (quotations from this page); Torrance, *Trinitarian Faith*, 230; Torrance, *Mediation*, xii–xiii; Torrance, *Preaching Christ Today*, 13, 14. Cf. Kye Won Lee, *Living in Union with Christ: The Practical Theology of Thomas F. Torrance*, Issues in Systematic Theology 11 (New York: Peter Lang, 2003), 146, 155, 165, 166, 188, 211, 212, 308, 309.

32. Torrance, *Divine and Contingent Order*, especially 97–112; Torrance, *Trinitarian Faith*, ch. 3; Torrance, *The Christian Doctrine of God*, ch. 8. Cf. Colyer, *How to Read T. F. Torrance*, 162–73.

33. Torrance, *Trinitarian Faith*, 230; cf. Torrance, *Incarnation*, 138, 139, 253.

34. Torrance, *Mediation*, 67–72, 81–6, 92–98 (quotation from 71, 95); Torrance, *The Christian Doctrine of God*, 153, 154; Torrance, *Atonement*, 189, 190, cf. 328, 329. Torrance warns of a "subtle form of Pelagianism" in evangelistic preaching that sees our salvation as ultimately conditioned upon our own repentance and faith rather than on Christ's work for us (Torrance, *Preaching Christ Today*, 35–39).

35. Colyer, *How to Read T. F. Torrance*, 120, 121.

36. *GCP*. Muller recognizes significant overlaps between Arminius and the Reformed theology of his generation as well as crucial differences. This analysis has been confirmed by Keith Stanglin, *Arminius on the Assurance of Salvation: The Context, Roots, and Shape of the Leiden Debate, 1603–1609*, Brill's Series in Church History 27 (Leiden/Boston: Brill, 2007), 13. See his summaries on pp. 111–13, 241, 242.

37. Hans Boersma, *Violence, Hospitality, and the Cross: Reappropriating the Atonement Tradition* (Grand Rapids: Baker Academic, 2004), 166, citing B. Loonstra, *Verkiezing-Verzoening-Verbond: Beschrijving en beordeling van de leer van het pactum salutis in de gereformeerde theologie* (The Hague: Boekencentrum, 1990). Arminius introduced this concept in his first oration, *Oration on the Object of Theology*, upon assuming his post at the University of Leiden in 1603; in *Works*, 1:321, 343, 344.

38. Stanglin urges that the major impetus for Arminius's assault on supralapsarianism was his encirclement by supralapsarians at the Uni-

versity of Leiden, not his youthful studies under Beza (*Arminius on the Assurance of Salvation*, 33, 34).

39. E.g., in *Dec. sent.*, in *Works*, 1:618–20, 623–25, 629–38, 647–53. Each of three authors of recently-published, reworked doctoral dissertations/ theses has claimed one of these three themes (God's character, Christ's significance, and Christians' assurance) as the mainspring of Arminius's theology: William den Boer, "Jacob Arminius: Theologian of God's Twofold Love," trans. Albert Gootjes, in *Arminius, Arminianism, and Europe*, 25–50; William den Boer, *God's Twofold Love: The Theology of Jacob Arminius (1559–1609)*, trans. Albert Gootjes, Reformed Historical Theology 14 (Göttingen and Oakdale: Vandenhoeck & Ruprecht, 2010); F. Stuart Clarke, *The Ground of Election: Jacob Arminius' Doctrine of the Work and Person of Christ*, Studies in Christian History and Thought (Milton Keynes and Waynesboro: Paternoster, 2006); and Stanglin, *Arminius on the Assurance of Salvation*.

40. Although cumbersome, the couplet "righteousness/justice" seems necessary in order to do justice to Arminius's conception, which includes both private morality and public (and even cosmic) order.

41. *Dec. sent.*, in *Works*, 1:623–25, 634–38; *Disp. pub.*, XIV.16; *Disp. priv.*, XX.4–6; XXI.3, corollaries, *Works*, 2:221, 222, 347, 348, 350, 352. See also *Disp. pub.*, XV.16 (*Works*, 2:229) on the pastoral applications of the doctrine of predestination. Stanglin, *Arminius on the Assurance of Salvation*, 219–31, 243, 244; den Boer, "Jacob Arminius"; and den Boer, *God's Twofold Love*, contribute in-depth treatments of the twofold love of God.

42. These are clearly presented in *Dec. sent.*, in *Works*, 1:653, 654, of which den Boer comments, "In this treatment of predestination in *Declaration*...Arminius appears to unite into a coherent whole all elements that are relevant to him. It is the most balanced exposition of Arminius' view on predestination that is available" ("Jacob Arminius," 47). Cf. *Disp. pub.*, XV; *Disp. priv.*, XL–XLI; Arminius, *Letter to Hippolytus* III; *Works*, 2:226–28, 392–95, 698–700). Except where noted, the remainder of this paragraph summarizes the outline in *Dec. sent.*

43. For the development of Arminius's understanding of the doctrine of predestination, see Clarke, *The Ground of Election*, 14–30. On the specific means of salvation listed above, see *Disp. pub.*, XVI.3–5, 11; *Disp. priv.*, XLI.8; XLII.2–4, 10; *Works*, 2:232, 234, 395–97.

44. *Dec. sent.*, in *Works*, 1:614–17.

45. *Dec. sent.*, in *Works*, 1:655; *Exam. Gom.*, Theses I and XXXII, in *Works*, 3:529, 651.

46. *Exam. Perk.*, in *Works*, 3:278–80; *Exam. Gom.*, Thesis XXX, in *Works*, 3:639–43.

47. *Dec. sent.*, in *Works*, 1:654.

48. *Disp. pub.*, IV.43–45; *Disp. priv.*, XVII.11–12; *Works*, 2:123, 124, 342. Cf. *GCP*, 154, 164, 270–75.

49. *Exam. Perk.*, in *Works*, 3:279 with *Oration on the Object of Theology*, in *Works*, 1:335. Carl Bangs's statement that "Arminius can be said to believe in absolute predestination—of Christ" (C. Bangs, 351) is true if "absolute" means "independent of any antecedent decree of predestination," but false if "absolute" means "unconditional."

50. *Oration on the Object of Theology*, in *Works*, 1:343.

51. *Exam. Perk.*, in *Works*, 3:434, 435.

52. Cf. *Exam. Gom.*, Theses XVII and XXIII, in *Works*, 3:574, 575, 590, 591.

53. *Dec. sent.*, in *Works*, 1:616.

54. *Exam. Perk.*, in *Works*, 3:324, 325.

55. Ibid., in *Works*, 3:328, 329; *Apology* on Article 12, in *Works*, 2:9, 10.

56. Here Clarke interprets Arminius as teaching that "Christ took upon himself the *fallen* human nature common to all" (*The Ground of Election*, 34, emphasis added)—that is, that the Son, by virtue of his incarnation, bore sin *ontologically*. While Arminius's comments could be construed in this manner if one reads them through Barthian spectacles, it is far more likely, given Arminius's Reformed scholastic context, that he agrees with Perkins that the Son assumed human nature *as such* rather than *as fallen* and bore sin *forensically*. See *Golden Chain*, chs. XII, XV–XVIII in *The Works of William Perkins*, ed. Ian Breward, The Courtenay Library of Reformation Classics 3 (Appleford: Sutton Courtenay, 1970), 191, 192, 199, 200. Of the many accusations with which Arminius had to contend, none involved advocacy of a fallen human nature in Christ—a position associated in following years in Holland with the sectarian mystic Antoinette Bourignon (1616–1680), as documented by Harry Johnson, *The Humanity of the Saviour: A Biblical and Historical Study of the Human Nature of Christ in relation to Original Sin, with special reference to its Soteriological Significance*, The New Lincoln Library series (London: Epworth, 1962), 137–39.

57. *Exam. Perk.*, in *Works*, 3:329–32. To Arminius's last two points, an objector could respond that God satisfies divine justice in the case of the reprobate by damning them and that God does not divorce particular redemption and irresistible grace but sovereignly wills that all for whom Christ died shall obey the gospel.

58. *Apology* on Article 12, in *Works*, 2:9.

59. Den Boer speaks of Christ's mediation as resolving a "'conflict'" between divine justice and mercy (*God's Twofold Love*, 115; inner quotation marks his).

60. *Exam. Perk.*, in *Works*, 3:328, 330–37; *Apology* on Article 12, in *Works*, 2:9, 10.

61. *Disp. priv.*, XXVIII.14; *Works*, 2:368.

62. *Apology* on Article 27, in *Works*, 2:52. In connection with this passage, Stanglin points out the distinctions among persuasion, irresistible

causality, and resistible causality (*Arminius on the Assurance of Salvation*, 80, 81n25). Den Boer perceptively remarks that "Arminius never appears to go farther than a double negative: grace is *not ir*resistible. Furthermore, it is not grace itself that is not irresistible, but rather the way in which grace works" (*God's Twofold Love*, 110; italics original).

63. Den Boer, "Jacob Arminius," 33, 50; den Boer, *God's Twofold Love*, 187, 194; cf. Stanglin, *Arminius on the Assurance of Salvation*, 87, 88.

64. Arminius gave two versions of this disputation, numbered *Disp. pub.* IX and X in *Works*, 2:162–89. This disputation's authoritative status for him is seen by his subsequent references to it in his *Apology* on Article 23, *Hippolytus* II, in *Works*, 2:35, 36, 692, and *Dec. sent.*, in *Works*, 1:658. Stanglin gives a detailed account of how public disputations at Leiden were conducted (*Arminius on the Assurance of Salvation*, 39).

65. *Hippolytus* II, *Works*, 2:696–98.

66. *Dec. sent.*, in *Works*, 1:657–64; *Apology* on Articles 17, 27, 28; *Disp. pub.*, XI; *Hippolytus* IV, in *Works*, 2:19, 20, 51–54, 189–96, 700, 701.

67. *Disp. pub.*, XVI–XVII; *Disp. priv.*, XLII–XLIV; *Works*, 2:230–42, 395–401; *Exam. Gom.*, Thesis XXXI, in *Works*, 3:646.

68. Den Boer, *God's Twofold Love*, 187, 188.

69. *Dec. sent.*, in *Works*, 1:628, 629. Stanglin points out that Arminius's university colleagues concurred that grace is not a force; they disagreed with him, though, by affirming its irresistibility. Arminius believed that the attribute of irresistibility would require it to be a force (*Arminius on the Assurance of Salvation*, 77, 81n27).

70. *Hippolytus* IV, in *Works*, 2:700, 701.

71. Torrance, *Mediation*, 94; McGrath records examples of Torrance's own practice in confronting the theological presumption of his students at Auburn Theological Seminary, USA, during the 1938–39 school year (*T. F. Torrance*, 54, 55).

72. Den Boer, "Jacob Arminius," 38, 39n36, and Clarke, *The Ground of Election*, 110, 158, appear to fall into this trap by trying to find hints in Arminius of Barth's view of Christ as the electing God. See also Clarke's reading into Arminius of Barth's view of Christ's fallen flesh, as previously noted. The parallelism of my statement above implies that Torrance was a Barthian—a claim that, like the identification of Arminius as Reformed, is controversial. See George Hunsinger, "Why T. F. Torrance was a Barthian," *Faith and Theology* (blog), December 20, 2008, http://faith-theology.blogspot.com/2008/12/george-hunsinger-why-t-f-torrance-was.html. See also the blog's banter by Princeton Theological Seminary doctoral students that led to Hunsinger's response. I use the term *Barthian* to refer to a theological descendant of Barth, not a would-be clone of him.

73. "It is not an overstatement to say that the architectonic concept holding together all of Torrance's thought is the unifying and eliminating

of theological-conceptual dualism" (Cassidy, "T. F. Torrance's Realistic Soteriological Objectivism," 193n102).

74. Torrance critiques federal theology for distinguishing among a covenant of redemption within the Trinity, a covenant of works and a covenant of grace (*School of Faith*, lxiii–lxiv).

75. This does not mean that Torrance ignores the righteousness of God. See *Atonement*, 99–108.

76. *Pace* Bangs, who claims regarding Arminius's rejection of irresistible grace, "There is the point: grace is not a force; it is a Person, the Holy Spirit, and in personal relationships there cannot be the sheer overpowering of one person by another" (C. Bangs, 343); and Olson, who repeats Bangs's claim and continues, "Arminius was concerned not only that God not be made the author of sin but also that the God-human relationship not be merely mechanical but genuinely personal." See Roger E. Olson, *Arminian Theology: Myths and Realities* (Downers Grove, Ill.: IVP Academic, 2006), 164. These statements anachronistically read into Arminius a post-Enlightenment interest in and refinement to the concept of personhood.

77. I have not discussed Arminius's denial to Christ of the unqualified title *autotheos* vs. Torrance's acceptance of this term, but the difference between them at this point is another example of Arminius's commitment to conditionality, causality, and distinction (the Son's deity is conditional upon and caused by the Father and so is distinct from the Father's deity in mode of origin) in contrast with Torrance's valuing of unconditionality, unity, and noncausality (the Son's deity is unconditioned by the Father and thus is the same as the Father's in being uncaused).

78. For a recitation of these struggles, see Jeremy Bangs's contribution to this volume, "Beyond Luther, beyond Calvin, beyond Arminius."

79. A longstanding tendency is to treat Arminianism as but an uncontracted spelling of Arianism. For Arminius's self-defense against the suspicion of Arianism due to his patristically supported scruples regarding applying *autotheos* to Christ, see *Hippolytus* I, in *Works*, 2:690–96. Precisely by attending to their particularities, Olson refutes the common accusations that associate Arminius and Arminians with Arianism and Pelagianism (*Arminian Theology*, 79–81).

80. See Reformed-Methodist International Dialogue, *Together in God's Grace* (Cambridge: World Alliance of Reformed Churches, 1987), http://ecumenism.net/archive/docu/1987_meth_warc_together_gods_grace.pdf.

81. *GCP*, 13, 19, 33, 34, 40, 41, 275, 280, 281. On pp. 154, 270–75, Muller claims that Arminius's doctrine of middle knowledge places him outside Reformed orthodoxy. Yet Muller also acknowledges that orthodox Reformed theologians, including Arminius's adversarial colleague Gomarus, accepted the concept (154, 164). Clearly, then, the true issue for Muller

is the specific *use* that Arminius made of the concept in order to support "his revision of the doctrine of predestination [away from unconditional double predestination] and...his soteriological synergism" (154). It is Arminius's affirmation of a universal divine salvific will and of resistible grace, not middle knowledge per se, that Muller sees as taking Arminius beyond the pale of true Reformed orthodoxy.

CHAPTER 7

WAS ARMINIUS AN OPEN THEIST? METICULOUS PROVIDENCE IN THE THEOLOGY OF JACOB ARMINIUS

John Mark Hicks

Ever since the emergence of open theism on the evangelical scene in the 1990s, there have been several attempts to saddle Arminianism with the theological interests of open theism.[1] On the one hand, Reformed theologians find it to their advantage to identify Arminianism and open theism, if for no other reason than the slippery slope or logical entailment argument has a concrete example. Open theists, on the other hand, seek some historical legitimacy through identification with Arminianism if not also some theological cover. As a result, whether one is seeking to delegitimize open theism (as some Reformed theologians intend) or to legitimize it (as some open theists intend), it is to the mutual benefit of Reformed theology and open theism to classify Arminianism and open theism together.

At one level all agree that there is a significant chasm between Calvinists and free will theists. Arminians and open theists stand together on one side of that abyss. Most agree that libertarian freedom is a significant part of that great divide.[2] Consequently, in a recent 4 *Views* book titled *Perspectives on the Doctrine of God*, Paul Helm and Bruce Ware represent Reformed ("Calvinist") positions whereas Roger Olson and John Sanders represent libertarian positions. Ware's introduction places Olson and Sanders in a "broad Arminian camp."[3]

Sanders no doubt appreciates Ware's classification. One of Sanders's interests has been to persuade the evangelical community that open theism is closer to a miniscule modification of Arminianism than a radical revision.[4] Indeed, Sanders seems to emphasize only two major differences, that is, the extent of divine foreknowledge and divine temporality.[5] Between these, claims Sanders, the main issue is the question of exhaustive foreknowledge.[6] But even then there "are *no practical differences*" between the two.[7] Neither Arminianism nor open theism questions the nature of foreknowledge as divine dependence upon contingent events—no matter what their understanding of divine temporality.[8] Open theism is actually, according to Sanders, "an attempt to correct some logical problems" that "are present in establishment Arminianism."[9] In fact, Sanders refers to his position as "open Arminianism."[10]

Olson does not dispute Sanders's minimalization of the differences between Arminianism and open theism.[11] While Olson disagrees with Sanders's conclusions concerning exhaustive foreknowledge, his essay does not note any other significant differences.[12] Olson does not exploit some of the key differences between the two positions even as he uses the language that would enable him to do so. For example, in contrast to theological determinism ("divine determinists") where God exercises "absolute, meticulous control of every twist and turn of every molecule," Arminians believe that "God *concurs* with every decision and action creatures make and do, but... does not cause all of it or control all of it."[13] This one concept—concurrence—pinpoints a key difference between classic Arminianism and open theism—that is, the theological notion of concurrence in relation to providential divine governance.

This chapter focuses on a specific difference between Arminius's theology and open theism, arguing that Arminius and open theists have significantly different understandings of God's providential activity. Meticulous providence is a phrase that is frequently, but loosely, used in discussions related to open theism. Reformed theology is typically described, rightly or wrongly, as a form of theological determinism, and this is often equated with meticulous providence. Sanders, for example, uses theological determinism and meticulous providence as practical synonyms. Even the self-styled Arminian Olson defines Reformed (monergism) theology as affirming "omnicausality, meticulous providence, and unconditional election or irresistible grace."[14] This use of meticulous providence is too delimiting and does not fully accord with the function of the term in other contexts. This chapter suggests, then, that meticulous providence, appropriately defined, is also a proper description of Arminius's understanding of divine providence.[15]

Defining Meticulous Providence

The philosopher of religion Michael L. Peterson was one of the first to introduce the phrase "meticulous providence" into contemporary philosophical discussions. He used it to clarify various responses to the evidential problem of evil, that is, the problem of the quantity, quality, and gratuitous character of evil in the world. He identified the "meticulous providence" principle as "an omnipotent, omniscient, wholly good God would not allow gratuitous or pointless evil."[16] The term, then, arose first in the context of philosophy of religion in the interest of theodicy. Peterson popularized this formulation through his 1982 book *Evil and the Christian God*.[17]

Meticulous providence is the denial of gratuitous or pointless evil. But what is gratuitous evil? John Hick called it "dysteleological evil" such that some events are "random and meaningless."[18] Philosophers of religion are constantly engaged in fine-tuning that definition. My concern, however, is not to settle any such discussion. Rather, I will only note that for Peterson—who inaugurated the use of this phrase—the meaning of gratuitous evil, defined in dependence on William Rowe, is whatever does not lead to a greater good.[19] In other words, meticulous providence assumes some form of "greater-good" theodicy.[20]

Subsequent discussion of the meticulous providence principle has expanded on Peterson. William Hasker, one of the contemporary "founders" of open theism, defined meticulous providence with more specificity in 1984: "*God exercises...a meticulous providence*—that is, a providence in which all events are carefully controlled and manipulated in such a way that no evils are permitted to occur except as they are necessary for the production of a greater good."[21] Hasker identifies not only the sense of "greater good" that is assumed by meticulous providence, but also characterizes the nature of that providence as "carefully controlled and manipulated."[22] Ultimately, Hasker includes both Reformed theology (which he calls theological determinism) as well as Molinism (which employs middle knowledge in its theological construction) in his definition. In a 1992 article he concluded that any system wherein every instance of evil is intentionally orchestrated by God toward the goal of some preordained good, either through decree or some form of foreknowledge (including middle knowledge), is a form of meticulous providence.[23]

Recently, following on the heels of Hasker, open theist and philosopher of religion Alan Rhoda has offered an even more specific definition of meticulous providence. He suggests the following formulation: "God is *either* an *ultimate sufficient cause* of everything that happens *or* (at least) *ordains* all things that come to pass."[24] In his definition, "ordain" does not necessarily mean that God directly causes an event or initiates a series of causes that determine an event. God may "weakly actualize" an event by causing a set of conditions which God knows will result in the event. This more nuanced definition includes, in his view, at least Molinism though it may exclude simple foreknowledge or timelessness depending on how those elements are construed. Molinism, both in its historic roots and in contemporary advocates, like Thomas Flint, has affirmed meticulous providence. For example, Flint writes, "God is sovereign in the sense that every event, no matter how large or small, is under God's control and is incorporated into his overall plan for the world."[25] In the current literature, Molinists are characterized as embracing meticulous providence even if some might think them inconsistent in doing so.[26]

In essence, meticulous providence in current philosophical theology entails at least two affirmations. First, no gratuitous evil exists—that is, every instance of evil serves a greater good. Second, God either directly or weakly actualizes every event in the world. More broadly, God thus governs the world in such a way that nothing happens without God's direct action or specific permission. Bruce A. Little, an Arminian who denies meticulous providence, summarized these points in this way: "God supervises every potential event of evil/suffering so that only those evils that can be used for God's good purposes are actualized."[27] Given this definition, open theists deny meticulous providence while Arminius himself would affirm it.

The definitions and uses of "meticulous providence" have morphed in the past thirty years. Originally, and still in the more technical literature of philosophical theology, the phrase described the denial of gratuitous evils. Presently, it has a more popular meaning—particularly promoted by open theists—that every event is determined by God in a traditional Reformed sense. In other words, "meticulous providence" has become synonymous with Reformed theology.

Consequently, it is not uncommon to find both Reformed and Arminian theologians classifying Arminius among those who would deny meticulous providence. Robert Peterson and Michael D. Williams, in their book *Why I Am Not an Arminian*, state that "Arminius rejected the Calvinist belief in meticulous providence and absolute predestination in which God's sovereign plan superintends and orders all things." This denial entails that "God's power and will are unabashedly circumscribed by the principle of human autonomy" with the result that Arminius's God "can get his way only if he happens to be traveling the same direction that we are."[28]

Even among Arminians there is a growing rejection of meticulous providence because it is associated with Reformed theology. Roger Olson, for example, regularly uses meticulous providence to describe Reformed theology and denies that Arminians believe it even though "many non-Reformed evangelicals tend to fall back on it as a default position in the face of calamities."[29] Other Arminians (or, sometimes self-styled Calvinians), however, affirm "meticulous providence."[30]

I suggest that one of the significant points of divergence between Arminius's theology and open theism *is* meticulous providence. Arminians who reject meticulous providence find themselves ultimately in a position similar to open theists, while those who affirm it will find themselves cuddling up to Reformed theology in perhaps unexpected ways.

THE OPEN THEIST DENIAL OF METICULOUS PROVIDENCE

John Sanders, whom I will use to represent open theism even though it is not a monolithic movement, tirelessly asserts that "when God decided to create beings with libertarian freedom God chose not to meticulously control them and this implies risk-taking for God," which, according to Sanders, is "affirmed by all Arminians."[31] Sanders rejects any notion that God has scripted the human drama or drawn up a blueprint for every act in creation. Free will theists reject theological determinism or, as it is often called in discussions of open theism, "meticulous providence."

Sanders contrasts "classical theism" (which for him is theological determinism) and "free will theism" on several counts, but I will focus on the one pertinent to my analysis of Arminius. According to Sanders, classical theists affirm "specific sovereignty"—that is, "only what God specifically ordains to occur actually happens." This is part of a "meticulous blueprint." Free will theists, in contrast, affirm "general sovereignty"—that is, "God ordains the structures of creation (our boundaries) and allows for human freedom (libertarian freedom)." Consequently, there is no "exercise of meticulous providence."[32] This appears in Sanders as an "either-or," as if these are the only two choices.[33] The net effect of general sovereignty is that God "macromanages" the creation though God may "micromanage" a few things.[34] Consequently, God does not have a "specific purpose for each and every event which happens" and thus Sanders denies that "each and every event has a specific divine intention."[35] As a result, general sovereignty "allows for pointless evil."[36]

General sovereignty, in contrast to specific sovereignty, means that while "God is in control in the sense of being accountable for creating this sort of world and carrying out the project the way God has" (i.e., "God alone is responsible for initiating the divine project and for establishing the rules under which the game operates"), God is not specifically responsible for any particular evil or tragedy.[37] God is "only...accountable for what he does intentionally," and this does not include what God permits under the conditions of the created order and the divine project.[38] God is responsible for the created reality as it stands, but God is not responsible for specific acts of evil within the creation.

The created order and libertarian freedom constitute key principles in God's governance of the world. Therefore, according to Sanders, "God could not prevent us from doing harm to one another without constantly violating the very conditions in which he created us to live."[39] Sanders seeks to preserve human freedom and divine goodness by removing God from any direct or specific responsibility for specific evils within creation. God cannot be responsible for evil except in some broad sense of general permission by virtue of the order of creation. God has no specific relation to any evil act. God is not responsible for particular acts of evil since God could not have prevented it without violating God's own creation order and intent.

This point is the fundamental theological and pastoral impulse of open theism. Sanders has stated it in multiple ways. The roots of his own theological reflection are the accidental death of his brother. "Was God responsible for my brother's death?" he asks.[40] Could God have prevented it? Or, worse, did God cause it? Sanders rejects meticulous providence because he believes that God bears no specific responsibility for evil acts in the world. One can hear Sanders's own experience as he recounts the relief others have felt in the light of open theism. This is the great service, according to Sanders, that open theism has rendered to many pastoral situations:

> The proponents of openness have concentrated on the problem of evil and many people find it liberating to not have to blame God for our evil and suffering. We do not have to think that God specifically ordained some horror for our supposed well-being. We do not have to pretend to be thankful for the evil that comes our way. Instead, we are liberated to fight against it, taking personal responsibility to collaborate with God (2 Cor. 6:1). Open theists have received thousands of letters and phone calls from people saying that they are so glad that they no longer have to believe God wanted their baby to die or their daughter to be raped.[41]

This impulse appears again and again in Sanders. For example, in the *4 Views* book he states it this way:

> This should relieve a great burden from many people who have been taught that everything that happens to us is part of the divine blueprint for the greater good. A fair number of people in church are angry at God though it is considered improper to confess it. The anger arises because people have been told to believe that God ordained their cancer or the death of a daughter for some unknown and difficult to grasp good.[42]

Sanders's theology of providence, then, has a pastoral impulse that arises out of his own experience. This is quite understandable as we all do the same thing as we seek to make sense of our own experiences of evil and tragedy. His theological interpretation of his experience, however, accentuates three significant differences between Sanders's version of open theism and Arminius's view of providence. At the heart of these differences is open theism's denial that God *specifically permits* every evil act, *concurs* with every finite act by acting alongside the actor and in the effects of the act, and sovereignly *directs* those acts toward good ends.

First, for Sanders there are "chance events and accidents" within the creation.[43] There are such events because God does not specifically permit every event. Sanders approvingly quotes Peter van Inwagen's definition of a "chance event" as any "state of affairs that is without purpose or significance" and "serves no end."[44] Human freedom and the boundaries of the created order mean that God permits random, accidental events: "Genuine accidents or unintended events, both good and bad, do happen, for that is the sort of world God established."[45] Divine permission entails that God gives "'consenting ontological support' to actions that he does not support morally"—which is equivalent to concurrence as ontological sustenance.[46] But this does not mean that God specifically permits evil acts or acts alongside of them in the sense of a teleological concurrence for each specific evil. Thus, tragic accidents and human horrors are fundamentally "chance" events even though there may be rare occasions when God "brings about" some "misfortune."[47]

Second, in consequence of chance events, there are gratuitous and pointless evils. These evils are gratuitous because they have no specific divine purpose. "The Holocaust is pointless evil," for example; or, "The rape and dismemberment of a young girl is pointless evil." And, Sanders adds, "The accident that caused the death of my brother was a tragedy." These events are pointless because "God does not have a specific purpose in mind for these occurrences."[48] Such tragedies or evils are "pointless because [they] do not serve to achieve any greater good."[49] There are events, then, within human experience that have no specific meaning or significance. They are simply accidents or, in the case of evil, monstrous horrors without purpose. Nevertheless, "God works to bring good out of evil," even if "God cannot *guarantee* that a greater good will arise out of each and every occurrence of evil."[50] Sanders's concern here is theodic, and it reflects the rising significance of the evidential version of the problem of evil within both pastoral and philosophical contexts (i.e., the quantity, quality, and gratuitous character of evil in the world) with which open theism is primarily concerned.[51]

Third, God has no specific sovereignty over all evil in the world. God is self-limited in terms of human evil. God "could," according to Sanders, "veto any specific human evil act, but if he made a habit of it, this would undermine the type of relationships he intends. God cannot prevent all the evil in the world and still maintain the conditions of fellowship intended by his purpose in creation."[52] God's hands are tied regarding specific occurrences of evil within the creation. "Most open theists" believe that "God does intervene at times," including Sanders.[53] But it raises considerable questions as to why God does or does not.[54] Consequently, open theists usually counsel that there are limitations to God's actions within the world. In raising the question of "why does not God [violate human freedom] more often in order to bring about a better world," Sanders points us to David Basinger who suggests "perhaps...God has already maximized the extent to which he may profitably violate human freedom."[55] The upshot is that God is doing the best God can. "We believe," Sanders writes, "that God is doing all he can, short of rescinding his original gifts of freedom to his creatures, to prevent what evil he can and, for that evil that does occur, God works to bring good out of those situations (Rom 8:28)."[56] But there are no guarantees that God will succeed, and presumably, whatever evil occurs is beyond God's sovereignty due to the creational boundaries God instituted—that is, God's own self-imposed limitations. God's sovereignty "cannot guarantee that a greater good will arise out of each and every occurrence of evil."[57]

Arminius on Meticulous Providence

I will approach the theology of Arminius through three lenses that are part of his theological world. Each of these provides a window through which we may see Arminius's affirmation of meticulous providence: (1) divine concurrence; (2) sovereign divine permission; and (3) divine governance. In effect, not only is Arminius a "greater-good" theodicist, but he also believes that God weakly actualizes all things in such way that God is sovereign over evil. God permits evil while also ruling over it.

Olson describes Arminius's notion of "divine concurrence" as "the most subtle aspect of his doctrine of sovereignty and providence."[58] It is most thoroughly discussed in the secondary literature by Richard A. Muller in *God, Creation and Providence in the Thought of Jacob Arminius*.[59] He argues that Arminius's theology of providence is a "modified Thomism" in response to the development of "early orthodox Reformed scholasticism."[60] Specifically, Arminius modifies early Reformed orthodoxy "with a distinctly Molinist view of divine concurrence."[61] This modification differentiates Arminius from his Reformed contemporaries, but it also embraces an understanding of concurrence that is antagonistic to open theism. This demands close attention because the implications are momentous.

Divine concurrence is a common assumption in Thomistic theology, as well as in the emerging Reformed scholasticism of Arminius's time. It affirms that God is the first cause of all finite acts. Through concurrence, God sustains finite reality, provides both the capacity and efficacy of creaturely actions, and specifically directs those actions toward the divine goal. In other words, God is the primary causal factor in every finite act—God sustains, effects, and directs everything.

Arminius modifies this understanding of concurrence. He maintains the notions of sustenance and direction, affirming that God ontologically sustains every act and directs (governs) every act. He modifies, however, efficacy. Specifically, in the divine permission of sin, "God suspends any efficiency (*efficientia*) possible to Him."[62] He writes,

> The last Efficiency of God concerning the Beginnings of sin, is the *Divine Concurrence*, which is necessary to produce every act; because nothing whatever can have an entity except from the First and Chief Being, who immediately produces that entity. The Concurrence of God is not his immediate influx into a second or inferior *cause*, but it is an action of God immediately [*influens*] flowing into *the effect* of the creature, so that the same effect in one and the same entire action may be produced [*simul*] simultaneously by God and the creature.[63]

Whereas traditional scholasticism affirmed a divine "influx" in the secondary cause such that God is a causal actor in every act, Arminius—following Molina, at least with regard to sin—places this efficacy in the effect rather than the cause. God simultaneously acts in the effect rather than "acting *in* or *on* the secondary cause." God effects the effects of sin rather than efficaciously causing the sin itself. For Arminius, as Muller notes, God acts "*with* the secondary cause and flowing, with it, into its action and effect." This protects the secondary cause as "determinative of its own action, and, therefore, free," while at the same time recognizing the simultaneous action of God.[64] God, as Arminius writes, "joins His own concurrence to the creature's influence"[65] and that concurrence "produce[s] an act."[66]

The difference between acting *in* and acting *with* a sinful act is the difference between theological determinism and libertarian freedom as it pertains to efficacy. Theological determinism attributes the primary efficacy to divine causation such that God causes the sinful action within the secondary cause. Arminius wants to avoid such a position because he thinks it makes God the author of sin. Consequently, Arminius argues that in the agent's determination to sin there is a suspension of divine efficacy along with a specific enabling permission of God. For Arminius, God ontologically sustains the secondary cause as the determinate cause, enables the capacity for secondary causation, and acts *with* the secondary cause rather than determining the secondary cause's action. Arminius rejects the notion that God is the primary (determinate) efficient cause in the sinful acts of the secondary agent because he wants to preserve both the freedom of the human will and the goodness of God who is not the author (cause) of sin.[67]

At the same time, while God permits evil, God actively performs the good. God is the ultimate cause in the performance of good such that all the glory for such goodness belongs to God. Arminius, therefore, affirms that "the power of God serves universally, and at all times, to execute these acts, with the exception of permission."[68] It appears, then, that the influx of power is universal except in the specific permission of moral evil: "For God does [effects] every good thing."[69] God concurs in sustenance, capacity, efficacy, and effect for humanity's good acts, but with regard to evil the divine efficacy is absent as a determinate cause since God does not cause moral evil.[70]

Rejecting theological determinism, Arminius nevertheless suggests a high view of providence that far outstrips anything imagined by open theism. For example, in every finite act, God acts with creation. This "with" means that there is no dimension of the finite creation where God is not active and simultaneously working toward the divine goal. Even when the action is sinful, God specifically permits the sin, concurs in its effect by acting alongside the agent, and directs it toward the divine goal. This does not mean that God approves of the act, in the sense of sanctioning it, but rather that God has sustained the act, has given the capacity to act, and has acted in the effects of the sin toward God's own purposes. Put another way, God has concurred in the act through permission and has thereby concurred (and acted) in the effect. In this sense, God effects the act but God is "permittor [sic] prior to being the effector."[71] God concurs and is thus the effector of the act, but the prior permission means that God is not cause of the sin. Arminius summarizes the point in this way:

> I openly allow that God is the cause of all actions which are perpetrated by His creatures. But I merely require this, that that efficiency of God should be so explained as that nothing whatever be derogated thereby from the liberty of the creature, and that the guilt of sin itself be not transferred to God; that is, that it may be shown that God is indeed the *effecter of the act*, but only the *permitter of the sin* itself; nay, that God is at the same time the effecter and permitter of one and the same act.[72]

God, as den Boer explains, becomes "the *effector* of the sinful act by joining his *concursus* to the influence of the creature, without which *concursus* an act would never come to pass."[73] Thus, God is both effector and permitter of the act, though permitter first.

This is not theological determinism but rather a sustaining and governing sovereignty. Arminius draws the contrast by commenting on a statement in the *Confession of the Dutch Churches* as he knew it:

> "Nothing is done without God's ordination," [or appointment]: If by the word "ordination" is signified "that God appoints things of any kind to be done," this mode of enunciation is erroneous, and it follows as a consequence from it, that *God is the author of sin*. But if it signify, that "whatever it be that is done, God ordains it to a good end," the terms in which it is conceived are in that case correct.[74]

Every finite act in the world, then, serves the divine goal and is ordained to a good end. Even sin, though it is not a good itself, can serve God's end whether "the creature intend the same end" or not.[75] Divine permission is "ordained...to a certain end, and that the best (*optimum*) end."[76] God uses even sin "for the end that he himself wills" and "does not allow the sin that he permits to lead to any end that the creature intends."[77] God, indeed, places a "limit on his permission, and a boundary on sin that it may not wander and stray *in infinitum* at the option of the creature." God prescribes the "time" and the "magnitude" of sin.[78] And thus "wisely, justly, and powerfully directs sin wherever he wills."[79] God both delimits and directs sin within the creation. God justly governs the creation in such a way that "all things" are "administered...to the best ends, that is, to the chastisement, trial, and manifestation of the godly—to the punishment and exposure of the wicked, and to the illustration of his own glory" and employs "that form of administration which allows intelligent creatures not only their own choice...to perform and accomplish their own motions and actions."[80]

Divine permission, then, is no mere general permission rooted in the created order. Rather, it is rooted in the divine will as it limits and directs sins though they are the free actions of human agents. Arminius stresses that "whatever God permits, he permits it designedly and willingly."[81] Divine permission, according to Arminius, is not merely general but quite specific. God decides to permit specific acts that could have been prevented or hindered. Consequently, "divine permission is not 'idle,'" inactive, or passive.[82] For example, "God permitted Ahab to kill Naboth" because "it was the divine will, that Ahab should fill up the measure of his iniquities, and should accelerate his own destruction." Or, "God permitted Satan and the Chaldeans to bring many evils on Job...for it was the will of God to try the patience of his servant." Or, "God permitted Judah to know Tamar his daughter-in-law...because it was the will of God, to have his own Son as a direct descendant from Judah."[83] Divine permission is a specific act of the divine will about specific events within the creation.[84] This is the case because God "places [*modum*] a measure or check on his Permission, and a boundary on sin, that it may not, at the option and will of the creature, wander *in infinitum*."[85]

God permits sin in general and any particular act of sin for two "general or universal reasons." On the one hand, God gave humanity a "freedom of the will" that was "designed as the mistress and the free source of their actions." On the other hand, there is the "declaration of divine glory" from which "the praise of the divine goodness, mercy, patience, wisdom, justice and power may shine forth and be revealed."[86] God permits the use of human freedom for divine glory, even when that freedom is used in malevolent ways. God does this because, as Arminius quotes Augustine, "God judged that it was the province of His most omnipotent goodness rather to produce good from evils, than not to allow evils to be."[87] At the same time, this glory is no egocentric self-adulation. God's glory *ad intra* is sufficient and needs no addition. God acts in the creation of the sake of his glory *ad extra* which includes the desire to commune freely with humanity. God permits sin for the sake of *ad extra* glory.[88]

Arminius's theology of providence involves no mere broad general permission of sin, but a concurrence in the ontology, capacity, and effect of the action itself. Divine providence, therefore, as Arminius defines it, "conserves, regulates, governs and directs all things, and that nothing happens by chance or accident" (*sed dico omnia eam conservare, regere, gubernare at que dirigere; quodque nihil plane casu aut fortuito contingat*).[89] Arminius does not believe that events within God's creation are independent of the divine will. Rather, God is intimately engaged with the creation in every one of its acts, even evil ones and, in this sense, divine providence is an expression of the will of God. Arminius's theology of providence does not allow for "accidental" or "chance" events. God grants specific permission (not just the general permission conditioned by the created order) for evil or tragedy and thus Arminius's understanding of providence is meticulous though it is not deterministic. In other words, every evil act is deliberately and specifically permitted. And every permission is given with divine intent. He writes,

> Beside this, I place in subjection to Divine Providence both the free-will and even the actions of a rational creature, so that nothing can be done without the will of God, not even any of those things which are done in opposition to it; only we must observe a distinction between good actions and evil ones, by saying, that "God both wills and performs good acts," but that "He only freely permits those which are evil." Still farther than this, I very readily grant, that even all actions whatever, concerning evil, that can possibly be devised or invented, may be attributed to Divine Providence Employing solely one caution, "not to conclude from this concession that God is the cause of sin."[90]

Divine Providence is sovereign over free will and "nothing can be done without the will of God." Evil is subject to the specific sovereignty of God. Nothing happens without God's own decision—a decision to permit sin and concur in its effects. God limits, directs, and concurs in the effect of evil, but God does so for the sake of divine glory (both justice and goodness) and toward the "best ends" of humanity.[91]

It is important to recognize that Arminius did not regard free sinful acts by human agents as autonomous spaces within the creation. Rather, these acts were bounded by God's own goodness. Arminius argues that since there is no order of evil that "pass[es] beyond (*excedere*) the universal order of that Good which is Chief," every act is ultimately "reduced to order by" the "Chief Good" and therefore "evil can thus be directed to good" through the "infinite Wisdom" and omnipotence of God. Even though "sin has exceeded the order of every thing created, yet it is circumscribed within the order of the Creator himself and of the Chief Good." Sin, therefore, is bounded by the goodness of God.[92] God is sovereign over evil and no evil can exist that does not serve God's own end. God does not permit sin to serve the ends of the sinner but rather "employs it to that end which He himself wills."[93]

Arminius envisions a world in which every act needs specific divine permission or causation, that is, where God ordains everything either strongly or weakly. It is a world where God effects every good and permits every evil for good ends. For Arminius, God is—in some sense—the primary cause of every act. For good acts God acts *in* as well as *with* the actor. For evil events God acts *with* secondary actors as God permits them to do evil. God's relationship to good and evil is asymmetrical. Arminius's main interest is to protect God's faithfulness to God's own love by attributing the origin of evil in the world to human freedom so that God is not the author (i.e., determinative cause) of sin, as well as to protect God's sovereignty over the created order. On the one hand, Arminius seeks to preserve God's goodness—to defend God against the charge of being the author of evil. On the other hand, he believes that God is specifically responsible for evil acts in the world since God specifically permits each one. God is sovereign over the creation such that God decides whether to permit every specific act of sin. God is meticulously involved in the world even if not deterministically involved.

This is the position of Classic or Reformed Arminianism as it appeared in the first decades of the seventeenth century. It appears in the Arminian Confession of 1621, primarily authored by Simon Episcopius. The Confession states, for example, that though sin does not "follow from God's permission as an effect from a cause," nevertheless "the actions that flow from disobedience," God "variously directs either to this or that object, and to some certain end, to whom and what he pleases."[94] The result of this divine permission and direction (governance) is that "nothing happens anywhere in the entire world rashly or by chance (*temere aut fortuito*)" since God is neither ignorant nor "idly observing."[95]

We may wonder how Arminius can affirm such meticulous providence while at the same time affirming a libertarian understanding of human freedom. At some points, as William Witt has pointed out,[96] it appears that Arminius is uncertain as to how that works:

> The mode in which God as the universal principle flows into his creatures, and especially the rational ones, and concurs in action with the nature and will of the creature, is approved by me, of whatsoever sort it may be, if it does not infer a determination of the will of the creature to one out of contraries or contradictories...I should wish it to be plainly and solidly explained how all effects and defects in nature and in the will, of all sorts universally, are by God's providence, and yet God is free from fault, all fault (if there be any) residing in the proximate cause.[97]

Arminius's interest is to preserve the righteousness of God as well as to preserve divine sovereignty. He wants to explore ways in which he can preserve both and he is dissatisfied with Junius's resolution.

Eef Dekker has argued that "the theory of middle knowledge is at the very core of Arminius' doctrine of divine knowledge," which Arminius had adopted at least by the time he assumed his professorship at Leiden.[98] In addition, Muller believes that Molinism influenced Arminius's formulation of his theologies of concurrence, human freedom, sufficient and efficacious grace, and predestination.[99] It may be that Molinism was ultimately Arminius's solution to this problem. Stanglin and McCall think so.[100] This comports well with William Hasker's insistence "that that there is a close connection between the ideas of meticulous providence and middle knowledge; so close, indeed, that meticulous providence *without* middle knowledge is difficult to conceive."[101]

CONCLUSION

I suggest that we no longer use the language of "meticulous providence" as an equivalent for "theological determinism" (what open theists think is the Reformed understanding of sovereignty). Originally the phrase "meticulous providence" identified a view of providence that denies pointless or gratuitous evils. This does not entail determinism or any understanding of eternal decrees, as in Reformed scholasticism. Arminius affirmed "meticulous providence" (without using the phrase) because he denied that gratuitous evil exists. God is sovereign over evil such that no evil will occur that does not serve God's purpose or to which God does not attach some specific meaning or significance. Nothing happens, according to Arminius, by chance or accident.

Arminius affirmed with Reformed theology a "meticulous providence" where God has sovereignty over evil such that no evil act is autonomous and uncircumscribed by God's intent for good.[102] God is sovereign in such a way that God concurs with the act itself and its effect has specific meaning and significance. This is a critical difference between classic Arminianism and open theism. Whereas Arminius asserted an understanding of concurrence that entails meticulous providence, open theism does not. This difference is no minor one since it reaches to the very core of why open theism, at least pastorally, arose as an alternative to Reformed theology and more traditional Arminianism. When classic Arminianism affirms "meticulous providence" (in the sense defined herein), this constitutes a radical disagreement with open theism. In terms of "meticulous providence," Reformed theology and classic Arminianism stand together.

On the other hand, classic Arminianism and open theism share a common conviction that human freedom is, in some sense, libertarian rather than compatibilist. God permits sin, but is not the primary cause of sin. In the permission of sin, according to Arminius, God does not concur in the efficacy of the act though God does concur in the ontology and capacity of the act. Here open theists and classic Arminians agree. Where they differ is that Arminius believed that God concurs in the effect of every act in such a way that God sovereignly limits and directs the ends of sin. Open theists do not believe God has accorded Godself that sovereignty since they think it inconsistent with the divine project. Classic Arminianism does not claim that theological determinism is a necessary precondition for the purposefulness and the meaningfulness of every human experience, even tragic evil.

It is important to recognize that Reformed theology and classic Arminianism share a common vision of God's meticulous providence over creation such that there is divine intent, meaning, and significance in every event. There are no gratuitous evils because God concurs in the effect of every human act. This entails that God directs that act toward good ends. Since open theism rejects such sovereignty, this constitutes a radical revision of classic Arminianism.

If this account of Arminius is correct, then Arminianism sides more with Reformed theology than it does with open theism. Arminius's theodicy is decidedly Augustinian. Consequently, it is inappropriate to identify open theism as a subspecies of a broad Arminianism. On the contrary, this is a fundamental difference in how Arminianism and open theism conceive divine providence and thus how they deal with theodicy.

Historically, Arminianism embraced meticulous providence as the best account of God's providence. Generally, contemporary (as opposed to classical) Arminianism has abandoned meticulous providence in the light of the evidential problem of evil and in this way became a midwife to the birth of open theism.

NOTES

1. A version of this chapter first appeared as "Classic Arminianism and Open Theism: A Substantial Difference in Their Theologies of Providence," *Trinity Journal* 33 (2012): 3–18. Used by permission.

2. Bruce A. Ware, *God's Lesser Glory: The Diminished God of Open Theism* (Wheaton, Ill.: Crossway Books, 2000), 220, 226.

3. Bruce A. Ware, "Introduction," in *Perspectives on the Doctrine of God: 4 Views*, ed. Bruce A. Ware (Nashville: B&H Publishing, 2008), 2.

4. John Sanders, "'Open Theism': A Radical Revision or Miniscule Modification of Arminianism," *Wesleyan Theological Journal* 38 (2003): 69–102. Cf. John Sanders, "Why Simple Foreknowledge Offers No More Providential Control Than the Openness of God," *Faith and Philosophy* 14 (1997): 26–40; and John Sanders, "Be Wary of Ware: A Reply to Bruce Ware," *JETS* 45 (2002): 221–31.

5. Sanders, "'Open Theism,'" 77–78.

6. John Sanders, "Responses to Roger Olson," in Ware, *Perspectives*, 182.

7. Sanders, "'Open Theism,'" 92 (italics original).

8. Steven Studebaker, "The Mode of Divine Knowledge in Reformation Arminianism and Open Theism," *JETS* 47 (2004): 469–80.

9. Sanders, "'Open Theism,'" 78.

10. Ibid., 90.

11. Olson defines "classical Arminianism" as a Protestant evangelical theology affirming the five points of the 1611 Remonstrance (to which the TULIP of Calvinism responds) and thus includes open theism within this definition. See Roger Olson, "Diversity of Calvinism/Reformed Theology," *Patheos* (blog), August 13, 2010, http://www.patheos.com/blogs/rogereolson/2010/08/diversity-of-calvinismreformed-theology/. In this sense, open theists may not differ from Classical Arminians, but this is neither the subject of this paper nor was it the topic of the 4 *Views* book. Further, the Remonstrance itself is insufficient as a definition of Arminianism.

12. Roger Olson, "Responses to John Sanders," in Ware, *Perspectives*, 248–51.

13. Roger Olson, "The Classical Free Will Theist Model of God," in Ware, *Perspectives*, 171 (emphasis added).

14. Roger E. Olson, "Confessions of an Arminian Evangelical," in *Salvation in Christ: Comparative Christian Views*, ed. Roger R. Keller and Robert L. Millet (Provo, Utah: Religious Studies Center, Brigham Young University, 2005), 190.

15. See Stanglin and McCall, 23, where they describe Arminius's view as "meticulous providence."

16. Michael L. Peterson, "The Inductive Problem of Evil," *Journal of the American Scientific Affiliation* 33 (1981): 85. Cf. Michael L. Peterson, "Evil and Inconsistency: A Reply," *Sophia* 18:2 (1979): 20–27.

17. Michael L. Peterson, *Evil and the Christian God* (Grand Rapids: Baker, 1982).

18. John Hick, *Evil and the God of Love* (New York: Harper & Row, 1975), 51.

19. William Rowe, *Philosophy of Religion: An Introduction* (Belmont, Calif: Dickenson, 1978), 89. Cf. William Rowe "The Problem of Evil and Some Varieties of Atheism," *American Philosophical Quarterly* 16 (1979): 335: "An instance of intense suffering which an omnipotent, omniscient being could have prevented without thereby losing some greater good or permitting some evil equally bad or worse."

20. Peterson, *Evil and the Christian God*, 75.

21. William Hasker, "Must God Do His Best?," *International Journal for the Philosophy of Religion* 16 (1984): 216–17.

22. It is unfortunate that Hasker uses such a pejorative term as *manipulated* to describe this view.

23. William Hasker, "Providence and Evil: Three Theories," *Religious Studies* 28 (1992): 99–101.

24. Alan Rhoda, "Gratuitous Evil and Divine Providence," *Religious Studies* 46 (2010): 283: "By 'ordaining' an event, I mean that God either strongly or weakly actualizes it. To 'strongly actualize' an event is to be an ultimate sufficient cause of it. To 'weakly actualize' an event is to strongly actualize conditions knowing for certain that they will lead to the event, despite the fact that those conditions are not causally sufficient for it."

25. Thomas Flint, *Divine Providence: The Molinist Account* (Ithaca, N.Y.: Cornell University Press, 1998), 13.

26. Steven B. Cowan, "Molinism, Meticulous Providence, and Luck," *Philosophia Christi* 11, no. 1 (2009): 158: "The Molinist typically accepts this meticulous view of divine providence. He believes that God had such a plan and that each day of human history constitutes the unfolding of that plan, a plan over which God exercises complete control."

27. Bruce A. Little, "God and Gratuitous Evil," (handout of a lecture at the annual meeting of the Evangelical Theological Society, San Francisco, Calif., 16–18 November 2011), 1. This lecture will be part of an unidentified forthcoming book.

28. Robert Peterson and Michael D. Williams, *Why I Am Not an Arminian* (Downers Grove, Ill.: InterVarsity, 2004), 111.

29. Roger Olson, *Westminster Handbook of Evangelical Theology* (Louisville: Westminster John Knox, 2004), 245. See, for example, Steve Lemke, "A Biblical and Theological Critique of Irresistible Grace," in *Whosoever Will: A Biblical-Theological Critique of Five Point Calvinism: Reflections on John 3:16*, ed. David Allen and Steve Lemke (Nashville: Broadman & Holman, 2010), 153, who opposes "meticulous providence."

30. Ken Keathley, *Salvation and Sovereignty: A Molinist Approach* (Nashville: Broadman & Holman, 2010), 21–27.

31. Sanders, "'Open Theism,'" 96–97.

32. Ibid., 71, 75.

33. John Sanders, *The God Who Risks: A Theology of Providence* (Downers Grove, Ill.: InterVarsity, 1998), 211–17.

34. Ibid., 213.

35. Ibid., 214.

36. Ibid.

37. Ibid., 215.

38. Ibid., 261.

39. John Sanders, "Openness and the Problem of Good and Evil," in *Does God Have a Future? A Debate on Divine Providence* (Grand Rapids: Baker, 2003), 41.

40. John Sanders, "How I Came to the Open View," in *Does God Have a Future*, 11. See also Sanders, *God Who Risks*, 9–10.

41. Sanders, "'Open Theism,'" 98–99.

42. John Sanders, "Divine Providence and the Openness of God," in Ware, *Perspectives*, 213–14. Used by permission. *Perspectives on the Doctrine of God: Four Views*, edited by Bruce Ware ©2008 B&H Publishing Group.

43. Ibid., 207, 213. See Sanders, *God Who Risks*, 215–16, 261–63.

44. Sanders, *God Who Risks*, 215–16, quoting Peter van Inwagen, "The Place of Chance in a World Sustained by God," in *Divine and Human Action: Essays in the Metaphysics of Theism*, ed. Thomas Morris (Ithaca, N.Y.: Cornell University Press, 1998), 220.

45. Sanders, *God Who Risks*, 216.

46. Ibid., 220, quoting Vincent Brummer, "On Thanking God Whatever Happens," *Journal of Theology for Southern Africa* 48 (1984): 9.

47. Sanders, *God Who Risks*, 216.

48. Ibid., 262.

49. Ibid.

50. Ibid., 263 (italics original).

51. Cf. Terence Penelhum, "Divine Goodness and the Problem of Evil," *Religious Studies* 2 (1967): 107: "It is logically inconsistent for a theist [one who believes in an omnipotent, omniscient and wholly good God] to admit the existence of a pointless evil." This is the theodic problem to which open theism is responding.

52. Sanders, "Divine Providence and the Openness of God," in Ware, *Perspectives*, 211. See Sanders, *God Who Risks*, 258–59.

53. Sanders, "Divine Providence and the Openness of God," in Ware, *Perspectives*, 212: "Additionally, in my opinion, God is much more active than we can ever identify; but most of his work, like an iceberg, goes unseen by us. God may be doing much in any given situation even if we do not detect it or if it is not the sort of help we desire."

54. Ibid., 211–12.

55. Ibid., there referring to David Basinger, *Divine Power in Process Theism: A Philosophical Critique* (Albany, N.Y.: State University of New York Press, 1988), 63.

56. Sanders, "Divine Providence and the Openness of God," in Ware, *Perspectives*, 213. It would seem, then, that God is severely limited since God could not even prevent the horror of the Holocaust much less other tragic events in life. Cf. Paul Kjoss Helseth, "On Divine Ambivalence: Open Theism and the Problem of Particular Evils," *JETS* 44 (2001): 493–511, particularly 507n48: "But if these kinds of evils or the potential consequences of these evils are not sufficiently egregious to warrant unilateral intervention, then what in the world could be? Are we *really* to believe that God has intervened in the past *only* when particular evils were

in the process of surpassing the wickedness of things even more egregious than child kidnappings and rapes, or the events that led to the Cultural Revolution or the Cultural Revolution itself?"

57. Sanders, "Divine Providence and the Openness of God," in Ware, *Perspectives*, 213.

58. Roger E. Olson, *Arminian Theology: Myths and Realities* (Downers Grove, Ill.: IVP Academic, 2006), 22.

59. *GCP*, 235–68.

60. Ibid., 268.

61. Ibid., 266. On Arminius's Molinism, see Eef Dekker, "Was Arminius a Molinist?" *Sixteenth Century Journal* 27 (1996): 337–52.

62. *Exam. Perk.*, in *Works*, 3:390.

63. *Disp. pub.*, X.9; *Works*, 2:183.

64. *GCP*, 255.

65. *Exam. Perk.*, in *Works*, 3:418.

66. Ibid., 3:398. Cf. William Lane Craig, "Response to Paul Kjess Helseth," in *Four Views of Divine Providence*, ed. Dennis W. Jowers (Grand Rapids: Zondervan, 2011), 57: "In Molina's view, God not only conserves both the secondary agent and its effect in being, he also wills specifically that the effect be produced, and he concurs with the agent by causing the intended effect. Without such concurrence, the effect would not be produced."

67. Arminius, "Letter Addressed to Hippolytus a Collibus," III, *Works*, 2:697–98: "I most solicitously avoid two causes of offense,—that God be not proposed as the author of sin—and that its liberty be not taken away from the human will: Those are two points which if anyone knows how to avoid, he will think upon no act which I will not in that case most gladly allow to be ascribed to the Providence of God, provided a just regard be had to the Divine pre-eminence."

68. *Disp. priv.*, XXVIII.8; *Works*, 2:367.

69. *Exam. Perk.*, in *Works*, 3:371. Also, "For He permits sin, but does [effects] good" (*Works*, 3:371).

70. This point is noted by J. Matthan Brown, "The Impact of Luis de Molina on Jacob Arminius," *Truth Is a Man* (blog), November 19, 2009, http://jmatthanbrown.wordpress.com/2009/11/19/the-impact-of-luis-de-molina-on-jacob-arminius/. Contra *GCP*, 236.

71. *Disp. pub.*, X.9; *Works*, 2:183.

72. *Exam. Perk.*, in *Works*, 3:415.

73. William den Boer, *God's Twofold Love: The Theology of Jacob Arminius (1559–1609)*, trans. Albert Gootjes, Reformed Historical Theology 14 (Oakville: Vandenhoeck & Ruprecht, 2010), 98.

74. *Dec. sent.*, in *Works*, 1:704–5.

75. *Disp. pub.*, IX.17; *Works*, 2:172.

76. *Exam. Perk.*, in *Works*, 3:390.
77. *Disp. pub.*, X.10; *Works*, 2:184.
78. Ibid., X.18; *Works*, 2:173.
79. Ibid., X.10; *Works*, 2:184.
80. Ibid., IX.23; *Works*, 2:177.
81. Ibid., IX.11; *Works*, 2:168; also *Disp. pub.*, X.5; *Works*, 2:180.
82. *Exam. Perk.*, in *Works*, 3:393.
83. *Disp. pub.*, IX.14; *Works*, 2:170.
84. As Gregory A. Boyd notes, this is precisely the position of Molinism: "The Molinist must accept that each and every *particular* evil was *specifically* permitted by God for a *specific* good reason" (italics original). This radically contrasts with open theism as Boyd articulates it: "In the open view, God has a morally justified reason for giving agents the capacity freely to engage in a certain range of *possible* behaviors but no specific reason for how agents use their freedom." See Boyd, "Response to William Lane Craig," in Jowers, *Four Views on Divine Providence*, 139.
85. *Disp. pub.*, X.11; *Works*, 2:184.
86. *Exam. Perk.*, in *Works*, 3:408.
87. Ibid.
88. See the discussion by Stanglin and McCall, 79–81, 130–31.
89. My own translation of *Opera*, 121 (cf. *Dec. sent.*, in *Works*, 1:657). It is important to remember that the Latin text is a posthumous translation of Arminius's Dutch original. Gunter (139) provides an English translation of the Dutch original: "I declare that providence defined in this way preserves, regulates, governs, and directs all things—for nothing in the world happens fortuitously or merely by chance."
90. *Dec. sent.*, in *Works*, 1:657–58.
91. *Disp. pub.*, IX.23; *Works*, 2:177.
92. *Disp. pub.*, IX.5; *Works*, 2:164.
93. *Disp. pub.*, IX.17; *Works*, 2:172.
94. *The Arminian Confession of 1621*, VI.3, trans. Mark A. Ellis (Eugene, Oreg.: Pickwick Publications, 2005), 60.
95. Ibid., 62.
96. William Gene Witt, "Creation, Redemption, and Grace in the Theology of Jacob Arminius," 2 vols. (Ph.D. diss., Notre Dame University, 1993).
97. Arminius, *Response to Junius*, 6, in *Works*, 3:366–67.
98. Dekker, "Was Arminius a Molinist?," 337. By noting the timing, Dekker is able to explain several agnostic statements about divine knowledge to Junius. For example, "Conference with Junius," *Works*, 3:64: "But the mode in which he knows certainly future contingencies, and especially those which appertain to creatures of free will, and which he has decreed to permit, not himself to do—this I do not comprehend, not even

in that measure in which I think it is understood by others of greater skill than myself." At one point, he found Thomistic "eternal presence" a possible explanation (*Conference with Junius, Works,* 3:62). William Gene Witt thinks Arminius's Molinism is possible but not likely. Cf. Witt, "Creation, Redemption, and Grace," 1:354–67.

99. *GCP,* 135–39, 162–63, 253–56.

100. Stanglin and McCall, 65–69.

101. William Hasker, *God, Time and Knowledge* (Ithaca, N.Y.: Cornell University Press, 1998), 203.

102. Sanders's version of libertarian freedom is fundamentally "autonomous," and he sometimes describes it that way; cf. Sanders, "Divine Providence and the Openness of God," in Ware, *Perspectives,* 231.

CONCLUSION

Arminius Reconsidered: Thoughts on Arminius and Contemporary Theological Discourse for the Church Today

Keith D. Stanglin

To "reconsider" Jacob Arminius, and, as the conference's original title suggested, to do so for the purpose of theology today, is a task that few have pursued in the last four centuries. When Protestants have engaged in historically informed systematic theology, with few exceptions, they have not done so in conversation with Arminius. Not only have Arminius's writings often been neglected,[1] but also the verdict on Arminianism—*pro et contra*—has been decided without need for further examination.

In recent years, scholars have begun to discover anew the "historical Harmenszoon."[2] These advances in scholarly, historical research, though, have not quickly influenced constructive dialogue in systematic theology. The goal of this book is to clarify further the historical picture and to move toward the theological implications, providing some possible models for how such historically sensitive theological dialogue might look. The intention in this conclusion is to reflect on some of the historical and theological themes that have emerged from the book's essays, and, in so doing, to make a case for retrieval theology in conversation with Arminius.[3]

Before contemporary theologians can begin a conversation with Arminius, they must learn his language. That is, one must attempt to understand Arminius and his writings on their own terms and in their historical context before attempting to evaluate or appropriate his thought. Simply by interacting directly with Arminius, the essays in the present volume have already advanced beyond many popular discussions of Arminianism. A few of these essays, echoing recent scholarship, have once again challenged some of the old myths about Arminius. For example, in their essays, Richard Muller and especially Tom McCall underscore that Arminius cannot be fully appreciated without giving attention to his academic context and his own use of scholastic method—even modal logic—to treat theological and philosophical questions. The historical Harmenszoon, as with history in general, is more varied and complex than most textbook accounts would have it.

Arminius's academic context: The University of Leiden, 1614.
Courtesy of The Leiden American Pilgrim Museum.

Another historical element that has not been as prevalent in recent scholarship, yet has surfaced in the essays by Jeremy Bangs and Stephen Gunter, is how rapidly and thoroughly Arminius was lost in the debates that followed his death, among both anti-

Arminians and Arminians. In a highly polemical age, the fact that Arminius's opponents would misread him should come as no surprise, for Arminius himself, while he was still alive, could scarcely quell the rumors and misrepresentations (willful or not) that were spread about his teachings and intentions. In 1608, for example, Arminius responded point by point to thirty-one propositions that were circulated falsely in his name. Needless to say, after 1609, Arminius was not around anymore to explain or defend himself, and his voice quickly receded into the background.

In addition to the complex political machinations that threatened to subordinate all theological motives (not only those of Arminius) in the 1610s, the explicit theological concerns of the Contra-Remonstrants leading up to the Synod of Dort were increasingly focused away from Arminius. During the second decade of the seventeenth century, Arminius's thought was directly treated, for the most part, only to the degree that it was accurately represented in the Remonstrance of 1610. Other controversies during Arminius's lifetime—on Christology or justification, for example—were mostly ignored in the later debates. For the Dutch Contra-Remonstrants and their international allies, Conrad Vorstius, would-be successor to Arminius's vacant chair of theology, became the bogeyman, whereas Arminius and all things Arminian simply were regarded as part of the Vorstian slippery slope. And since Vorstius's theology was undeniably a development beyond that of Arminius, Arminius's actual theology was obscured in the discussions though his name was continually invoked. Even after the Remonstrants distanced themselves from Vorstius, it was the Remonstrants, not Arminius, who were most frequently being read and assessed by the Contra-Remonstrants and Synod of Dort.

Not only was there a tendency for the Contra-Remonstrants to lose sight of Arminius, but Arminius was also supplanted among the supposed Arminians. To be sure, some Remonstrants, such as Johannes Corvinus, undertook the defense of Arminius's treatises against opponents, but such expositions are by definition removed from Arminius. More frequently, Remonstrants such as Peter Bertius, Johannes Uytenbogaert, Hugo Grotius, and Simon Episcopius were understandably more concerned with articulating their own views than with defending Arminius. And the later Remonstrant positions on religious epistemology, Scripture, Trinity, atonement, and soteriology were noticeably out of step with the views of Arminius. Later Anglican and Wesleyan "Arminianisms," which have no direct genealogical relationship to Arminius, often failed to interact with Arminius as well. The notion of "Arminius versus the Arminians"—that there is a comparatively deep discontinuity between the content of Arminius's theology and that of later Arminians—stands on much firmer ground than the old "Calvin versus the Calvinists" hypothesis.

That theologians such as Grotius, Episcopius, and Fletcher would go their own ways is neither improper nor unexpected. Just as later Reformed theologians were no slavish followers of Calvin, Remonstrants and Methodists were not trying to mimic Arminius. The historical and perhaps theological problem, however, is that these and other later thinkers are regarded unqualifiedly as "Arminian." To the extent that Remonstrants and Wesleyans have been classified as Arminian, Arminius's theology became confused with theirs. Arminianism, as a catchall term for anti-Calvinism, has since come to mean anything from high church Anglican order to Pelagianism to open theism. Depending on one's outlook, then, Arminius is, to his admirers, the champion of toleration, free will, and biblical, nondogmatic theology, or, to his detractors, the advocate of anthropocentrism and incipient heresy. Most of these perspectives are, at best, one-sided caricatures that have only a tenuous connection to Arminius himself.

However the dialogue should proceed, our contention is that Arminius is a figure well worth retrieving for contemporary theological and ecumenical discourse, and his works should be part of a Protestant and evangelical *ressourcement*. To this end, attention must be paid to the widely available writings of Arminius, and progress must be made toward publishing original-language and translated editions of his many writings that have never been published or used.

Reading and learning from the other side is one obvious way to initiate fruitful dialogue. It is safe to say that more "Arminians" have read Calvin than "Calvinists" have read Arminius. Certainly the writings of and information about Calvin are more readily accessible than those of Arminius, but the existing primary and secondary sources on Arminius have not been sufficiently utilized. Once the resources and ideas have been seriously engaged, rather than passing on the caricatures and misunderstandings about Arminius, Calvinists should challenge and correct them. Arminians should do the same for Calvin and Reformed theology.

In seeking to retrieve and appropriate Arminius for today, the goal is not to repristinate his theology. No one would likely want to advocate everything that Arminius or that his contemporaries believed. At the same time, it would be equally nearsighted to reject everything that they said simply because they, for example, held to an older metaphysics or embraced a precritical view of Scripture. In fact, the failure of modern theology to reach a consensus on a replacement metaphysics and the increasing disenchantment with modern exegesis may imply that Arminius and his contemporaries are more timely now than in recent memory. At any rate, the point is to distinguish Arminius from vague notions of Arminianism and then to permit him to be a conversation partner on his own terms.

In addition to more informed interaction with Arminius, another aspect that constructive current dialogue ought to face is the reality of the resurgence of the alleged "New Calvinism," the "young, restless, and Reformed." The Calvinist resurgence is being felt acutely in the Southern Baptist Convention, but it has also spread among many evangelical and nondenominational churches. I have taught in schools affiliated with Restorationist churches, a fellowship which traditionally has been very ahistorical in the quest to go back to the Bible. As a result, although these churches are exclusively Arminian (if not semi-Pelagian), most of my students did not grow up ever hearing about either Calvinism or Arminianism. Nevertheless, the unsolicited questions and concerns I continue hear from students in class and in my office over these classic debates reflect the resurgence. I believe such questions and the general awareness among students have increased over my ten years of teaching.

Why is there a resurgence of Calvinism? Evangelicals who have been deprived of deep theological reflection and a sense of confessional tradition and historic community have found what they are looking for in various Christian traditions: in Eastern Orthodoxy, in Roman Catholicism, and, for those who still think there was something to the Protestant Reformation, in Reformed theology. As has often been noted, in addition to its logical consistency and ability to explain some otherwise difficult passages of Scripture, Reformed theology also boasts very persuasive proponents and popularizers. The brand of Calvinism that is resurging is often not classic Reformed orthodoxy, but a form of metaphysical pandeterminism influenced by American evangelicalism. Arminianism, on the other hand, may be enjoying a mild resurgence as a reaction to this version of Calvinism. And this popular rise in so-called "Classical Arminianism" has unfortunately been largely untouched and unaffected by the scholarly resurgence that has been occurring in Arminius studies over the last couple of decades.

These popular resurgences have had some negative consequences. A simple Internet search for "Calvinism" or "Arminianism" will reflect the negativity. The online discourse is too frequently found wanting in both historical and theological literacy as well as Christian charity. The admirable quest for greater understanding of ourselves and one another too easily turns into obsession with what is wrong with the other. "For Calvinism" quickly devolves into "against Arminianism" or "against heresies," and vice versa. The distinction between "for Arminianism" and "against Calvinism" is subtle, which makes the challenge of how to proceed all the more difficult.

In advocating current Christian dialogue in conversation with Arminius, we do not mean to suggest that Arminius was a mediating figure in his own day. In many important ways, his theology took a different trajectory from what was becoming Reformed orthodoxy, and on many questions related to the doctrines of God, creation, and salvation, there is honestly no common ground. With good reason, those conversations have taken place and those books highlighting the differences have been written many times over. In contrast, the present book and the kind of conversation it promotes are simply a departure from the exclusive "Calvinism versus Arminianism" paradigm.

Thus the essays in this book offer some hints as to how an informed and fruitful dialogue may proceed and how—or at least why—Arminius may be worth reconsidering. One may note, for example, the possible convergences that emerged. As Crisp and Van Kuiken point out, Arminius is more Reformed, or traditionally orthodox, than Jonathan Edwards and T. F. Torrance in key points of theology. If Edwards and Torrance fall under the Reformed umbrella and are widely regarded as dialogue partners for contemporary Reformed theology, why is Arminius automatically excluded from the conversation? And, as Hicks demonstrates, Arminius's doctrine of providence is quite different from, and certainly much more Reformed than, that of open theism. Indeed, open theism is more properly Vorstian than Arminian—it is Trinitarian but advocates divine mutability and presentism. Muller's essay indicates Arminius's role as a contributor to Reformed covenant theology. There may be more similarity between Arminius's views and the Reformed views on free will than previously thought. What other correlations might there be? Just as Protestants of all stripes have learned from Augustine, Anselm, and Aquinas with great profit without endorsing everything they said, it seems that Arminius could be granted a seat at the table as well. Even when one side cannot agree with the other, the concerns of each should be heard and respected.

The challenge of this discussion is the same one that has faced the old discipline of comparative dogmatics and the project of ecumenism at large. On the one hand, greater understanding can lead to heightened rhetoric and deeper division. But, on the other hand, more informed disagreement can also lead to greater appreciation of the differences and the commonalities. So, in addition to focused discussion and vigorous debate about predestination, perseverance, and the like, those who confess with the historic church the rule of faith summed up in the Apostles' and Nicene Creeds should give equal attention to how we can make our way forward, together, to face the challenges of the third millennium that confront all of us who wear the name of Christ.

NOTES

1. Reasons for the neglect of Arminius are discussed in Stanglin and McCall, 3–6.

2. For a survey of recent literature to 2009, see Keith D. Stanglin, "Arminius and Arminianism: An Overview of Current Research," in *Arminius, Arminianism, and Europe: Jacob Arminius (1559/60–1609)*, ed. Th. Marius van Leeuwen, Keith D. Stanglin, and Marijke Tolsma, Brill's Series in Church History 39 (Leiden: Brill, 2009), 3–24.

3. On retrieval theology, see John Webster, "Theologies of Retrieval," in *The Oxford Handbook of Systematic Theology*, ed. John Webster et al. (New York: Oxford University Press, 2007), 583–99.

CONTRIBUTORS

Jeremy Dupertuis Bangs is founding director of the Leiden American Pilgrim Museum in Leiden, the Netherlands.

Mark G. Bilby is a reference librarian at the Claremont School of Theology.

Oliver D. Crisp is professor of systematic theology at Fuller Theological Seminary.

W. Stephen Gunter is associate dean for Methodist studies and research professor of evangelism and Wesleyan studies at Duke University Divinity School.

John Mark Hicks is professor of theology and history at Lipscomb University.

Mark H. Mann is associate professor of theology and director of the Wesleyan Center at Point Loma Nazarene University.

Thomas H. McCall is associate professor of biblical and systematic theology and director of the Carl F. H. Henry Center for Theological Understanding at Trinity Evangelical Divinity School.

Richard A. Muller is P. J. Zondervan Professor of Historical Theology at Calvin Theological Seminary.

Keith D. Stanglin is associate professor of Scripture and historical theology at Austin Graduate School of Theology.

E. Jerome Van Kuiken is assistant professor of religion and philosophy at Oklahoma Wesleyan University.

www.ingramcontent.com/pod-product-compliance
Lightning Source LLC
Chambersburg PA
CBHW012128010526
44113CB00041B/2649